A Companion Guide to the National Gallery of Scotland

NATIONAL GALLERIES OF SCOTLAND
EDINBURGH · 2000

Published 2000 by the Trustees
of the National Galleries of Scotland

© The Trustees of the National Galleries of Scotland
ISBN 1 903278 11 2

Designed and typeset in FF Quadraat by Dalrymple
Printed in Belgium by Snoeck-Ducaju & Zoon

Frontispiece: The west suite of rooms in the
National Gallery of Scotland

Foreword

In recent years the National Galleries of Scotland have become increasingly active in organising major loan exhibitions, yet we have been equally active in expanding our permanent collections and making them better known. Besides making many outstanding additions to our collections we have also published concise, illustrated catalogues of the works belonging to the National Gallery of Scotland, the Scottish National Portrait Gallery and the Scottish National Gallery of Modern Art.

This fully-illustrated *Companion Guide to the National Gallery of Scotland* complements the two volumes already published on the collections of the Scottish National Portrait Gallery and the Scottish National Gallery of Modern Art. Lavishly illustrated, informative and reasonably priced, these books will, we trust, allow more people to share in the enjoyment of our collections, and encourage more and more to visit the National Galleries of Scotland.

TIMOTHY CLIFFORD
Director, National Galleries of Scotland

Fig.1 Proposed scheme for the interior of the National Gallery, c.1937–8
Oil sketch by Stanley Cursiter

Introduction

The National Gallery of Scotland enters the twenty-first century widely regarded as one of the finest smaller galleries in the world. Its collections range from c.1300 to c.1900 and include paintings, prints and drawings and sculpture. Within its elegant neoclassical exterior, designed by William Henry Playfair (1790–1857), one of Scotland's most accomplished architects of the nineteenth century, are housed works by the greatest names in Western art including Raphael, Titian, El Greco, Velázquez, Rembrandt, Rubens, Watteau, Tiepolo, Canova and many of the Impressionists and Post-Impressionists. The Gallery also contains the most comprehensive collection of Scottish art from the seventeenth to the nineteenth century with masterpieces by such well-known figures as Ramsay, Raeburn and Wilkie, as well as a host of less familiar names who all made their own contributions to one of the most distinctive of the smaller national schools. Furthermore, its graphics collection of just under 20,000 works is the finest in Scotland. Above all, the National Gallery's collection is distinguished both for the quality and for the interest of its holdings. Many artists are represented by particularly memorable examples, be it an unusual religious Vermeer, *Christ in the House of Mary and Martha* or an untypical early Monet, *A Seascape, Shipping by Moonlight*.

This combination of the remarkable allied to the excellent is pursued in the current acquisitions policy which has seen the recent arrivals of paintings by Guercino, Botticelli and Murillo and the addition, over the last two decades, of drawings by Seurat, Leonardo and Raphael among many others. Certain areas have also been specifically built up including French landscape painting, decorative prints and drawings, and medals and plaquettes.

Much of this institutional collecting is allied to a high degree of financial acuity whereby maximum advantage is taken of favourable tax conditions for works of art offered for sale, and frequent use is made of the tax in lieu and private sale facilities available under current legislation. Extremely generous grants from bodies such as the National Heritage Memorial Fund, Heritage Lottery Fund, National Art Collections Fund and the Pilgrim Trust have ensured that we have often been able to achieve quite spectacular 'gearing up' of our own purchase monies in pursuit of acquisitions which seemed far outwith our financial means. Our purchase funds, currently just under £1.3 million and voted to us by government, have to be shared with our sister institutions, the Scottish National Portrait Gallery and the Scottish National Gallery of Modern Art, which opened in 1889 and 1960 respectively. Together we fulfil for Scotland the roles carried out in London by the National Gallery, National Portrait Gallery, Tate Gallery (now 'Britain' and 'Modern') and the graphics departments of the British Museum and the Victoria and Albert Museum, albeit on a reduced scale.

It is normal practice for the introductory histories of institutions such as the National Gallery of Scotland to be given in chronological order. In this instance, however, it may be amusing and instructive to conduct this exercise in reverse, in effect to journey back from the present to the beginning. So, rather like the final movement of Haydn's *Farewell Symphony*, where the players gradually leave the stage until only the muted sounds of two violins can be heard, we shall eventually arrive at that moment, on the 30 August 1850, when the foundation stone of the National Gallery was laid by Albert, Prince Consort. This great event, from which

Queen Victoria tactfully absented herself, took place on the site chosen for the Gallery on the Mound in the heart of Edinburgh, overlooked by the castle and adjacent to Playfair's other great temple for the arts, the building now known as the Royal Scottish Academy, with whose history that of the National Gallery has been inextricably linked.

The cyclical nature of taste is nowhere better illustrated than in the present interior layout and decoration of the National Gallery for, with its red walls, green flooring and pictures very often arranged in two or sometimes three tiers, it is a conscious evocation of the original scheme as devised by Playfair's friend and colleague, David Ramsay Hay, who was also responsible for the Victorian interiors of the Palace of Holyroodhouse. The recent restoration (frontispiece) of the original decor of the National Gallery was carried out at the end of the 1980s. It replaced a fundamental redesign of the Gallery in the 1930s under the then Director, Sir Stanley Cursiter, whereby Playfair's round-arched divisions between the main ground-floor rooms made way for more formal room dividers in the shape of entablatures allied to Corinthian columns. Cursiter was both a distinguished director and painter, and he recorded his various proposals for the National Gallery interior in a series of oil sketches (fig.1).

As the collection of the Gallery has grown over the years, the need for more space has become increasingly urgent. The most recent expansion took place in the 1970s with the addition of what is now known as the 'New Wing'. This semi-underground structure, recipient of an award from no less a body than the British Concrete Society (!), provided additional space for offices, a library, print room and the rooms where the Scottish School paintings are normally displayed. Situated astride Playfair's railway tunnel, but below the eastern foundations of the National Gallery, this modest yet rather straight-laced addition represents a triumph of engineering, if not of aesthetics. It has suffered since its completion from the difficulties of fulfilling a dual function: not only must it house the previously listed facilities, but it also has to serve on occasion as our more substantial temporary exhibition space. Since its creation it has played host to many successful shows including The Discovery of Scotland (1978), Degas 1879 (1979), Lighting up the Landscape (1986), Cézanne and Poussin (1991) and Monet to Matisse (1994). Its versatility is its failing, however, and our current major project is to restore and upgrade the building of our neighbouring institution, the Royal Scottish Academy, so that it will be able to host our most important exhibitions and thereby leave the permanent collection in the National Gallery relatively undisturbed.

Although the rather uninspired architectural language of the 1960s and 1970s produced the New Wing, this was also a period of great enrichment of the collection, notably the magnificent gift and bequest of 1960 and 1965 of Impressionist and Post-Impressionist paintings from Sir Alexander Maitland. The rooms where these are now housed are among the most visited in the Gallery and include masterpieces by Monet, Van Gogh and Cézanne. Prior to this extraordinary largesse, the major examples of Impressionist and Post-Impressionist art in the collection had been Degas's great portrait of the Florentine art critic, Diego Martelli, and Gauguin's The Vision after the Sermon. They were brilliantly acquired by the Gallery in 1932 and 1925 respectively, in an era when British public collections were only just beginning to purchase such works. Cursiter and directors after him worked closely with the Maitlands and were acutely aware of the great and growing collection in the Maitland's house in Heriot Row, Edinburgh, which was ultimately destined for the National Gallery of Scotland. Indeed, on one occasion, recorded in Cursiter's privately published autobiography, the National Gallery committee refused to sanction the purchase of Gauguin's *Three Tahitians*. Instead, it was acquired by the Maitlands on the private understanding with Cursiter that it would one day find its way to the National Gallery, as indeed it did.

Ten years prior to Maitland's bequest of 1965 the Gallery had bought, in 1955, Velázquez's great early painting, *An Old Woman Cooking Eggs*, from the Cook collection for £57,000. This marked the Gallery's most expensive purchase to date. For the first fifty-three years of its existence the Gallery had managed with no annual purchase grant from government and such a facility was only established in 1903 when the Gallery was voted £1,000 per annum for this purpose.

Many of the masterpieces in the Gallery have come not by purchase, however, but by gift or loan. And nothing in the last category surpasses the magnificent Duke of Sutherland loan that came to the Gallery in 1945 at the end of the Second World War. This includes five Titians, two Raphaels, a Rembrandt self-portrait, and Poussin's second set of the *Seven Sacraments*. Their former home had been Bridgewater House in London, the picture gallery of which had been severely damaged by German bombing during the war. The majority of the pictures in the loan had originally been acquired by the 3rd Duke of Bridgewater when they appeared on the London art market in the wake of the French Revolution. Many of them came from the celebrated collection of the Duc d'Orléans formed at the beginning of the eighteenth century.

Two of the most significant acquisitions made by the Gallery in the first half of the twentieth century were Sargent's *Lady Agnew of Lochnaw* and Constable's *Vale of Dedham*, bought in 1925 and 1944 respectively. Both were acquired with the aid of funds left to the Gallery in 1919 by James Cowan Smith. Suitably reinvested, these greatly supplemented the relatively meagre annual purchase grant. Cowan Smith was an émigré Scot who spent much of his life in England in the Rotherham area. He apparently had no children but was immensely fond of dogs, and one of the conditions of his bequest was that a portrait by John Emms of one of his favourite dogs, a Dandie Dinmont called Callum, should be hung in the National Gallery of Scotland. This condition has been honoured, with the result that both Emms and Callum enjoy more exalted artistic company than either could realistically have expected.

In the years prior to the First World War the Gallery underwent great constitutional and physical change. The National Gallery of Scotland Act was passed in Parliament in 1906 and a separate Board of Trustees was created. This replaced the arrangement whereby the Gallery had been managed, since its founding in 1850, by a body known as the 'Board of Manufactures', an abbreviation of the 'Honourable Board of Trustees for Fisheries, Manufacturers, and Improvements in Scotland'. This had its origins in the Act of Union of 1707 and was established to improve the hemp and woollen manufactures and fisheries in Scotland. In 1760 it founded in Edinburgh the Trustees' Academy, an art school originally concerned with raising the level of Scottish textile design. By the early nineteenth century its main activities were in the field of the fine arts.

The situation regarding the housing of various bodies connected with the arts in Edinburgh at the time of the National Gallery of Scotland Act of 1906 was extremely complex. In many ways the Act and its subsequent Parliamentary Order of 1910 represent the most crucial watershed in the history of the National Gallery of Scotland. They were intended to disentangle the somewhat haphazard nature of what had gone before and to establish a proper constitution and governance for the Gallery.

The present-day visitor would no doubt be surprised to learn that until 1910 the Gallery building accommodated joint occupants, the eastern half being taken up by the Royal Scottish Academy and its collection and teaching facilities, the western half by the National Gallery. Both bodies had expanded considerably since the building had first opened to the public in 1859. And so a deal was done, under the terms of the 1910 Order, whereby the Academy transferred its collection of Old Masters to the National Gallery and removed to the adjacent building, originally known as the Royal Institution, but thenceforth as the Royal Scottish Academy. Both buildings were extensively remodelled at this time by a government architect, William Thomas Oldrieve (1853–1922), in works completed by 1912.

It was the Board of Manufactures who had paid for the construction of the building now known as the Royal Scottish Academy, but originally called the Royal Institution. In effect the predecessor of the National Gallery of Scotland, it had also been designed by Playfair. When it first opened in 1826 it housed the Trustees' Academy, the Scottish Society of Antiquaries, the Royal Society of Edinburgh, and the Institution itself. Exhibitions of contemporary art and Old Masters were held on these premises, which were enlarged to their present size and appearance in the 1830s. Needless to say, the increasing demands on this building's finite spaces led to the call for and construction of its distinguished neighbour, the National Gallery of Scotland.

If we could travel back to the Gallery's earliest years, after its opening in 1859, we would find a curious but promising mixture of works of art on show. The Royal Institution's pictures formed, in effect, the founding collection. In addition to the work of contemporary Scottish artists, it included 'ancient pictures', the most notable of which were Van Dyck's *The Lomellini Family* and *St Sebastian*, both originally acquired in Genoa by Andrew Wilson, Master of the Trustees' Academy, and Tiepolo's *The Finding of Moses*. Also on view was the Torrie Collection, comprising a number of important Italian and Dutch pictures including Jacob van Ruisdael's *The Banks of a River*. This had been formed by Sir James Erskine of Torrie (1772–1825) and was entrusted to Edinburgh University in 1835, but responsibility for its display was passed on to the Board of Manufactures in 1845. Two years after the National Gallery opened it received in 1861 the bequest of Lady Murray of Henderland, which included a number of outstanding French eighteenth-century pictures by masters such as Watteau and Greuze. Among other distinguished arrivals in the nineteenth century were Rembrandt's *A Woman in Bed*, presented by the brewer William McEwan in 1892, and John 'Spanish' Philip's *'La Gloria': A Spanish Wake*, the Gallery's most expensive purchase to date in 1897 at a price of 5,000 guineas.

In 1904 there appeared in the *Art Journal* a series of articles on the collection by the dealer and critic David Croal Thomson. This was doubtless occasioned by the government committee of inquiry charged with looking into the affairs of the Gallery's governance that resulted in the National Gallery of Scotland Act of 1906. Croal Thomson described a public that existed before Edinburgh became the centre for international tourism that it is today:

There is no institution in all Scotland better known to the Scots people themselves than the national gallery in Edinburgh. And this not only to the best educated portions of the community, but also to the lower middle classes and to the ordinary working people. All year round visitors are passing the turnstiles; even on dark winter days, when the light scarce

Fig.2 *Computer simulation of John Miller and Partners' plans for The Playfair Project,*
2000

reaches the clearness of a calm summer evening's 'gloaming,' I have seen a score or more people
trying to fathom the quality of the pictures; while on autumn mornings, when all the
residents in Scotland seem, in detachments, to visit their metropolis, the rooms are so crowded
as to be often quite full.'

He continued by praising the running of the Gallery:

There is also, no doubt, greatly owing to the fact that the Scottish National Gallery is one
that is now thoroughly well managed. The most is made of its somewhat slender sources of
display, and the works are so well arranged, and their quality so interesting, that it takes a
fairly liberal education to appreciate them with exactitude.

The Gallery had been administered, until then, by artists rather than curators
in the modern sense. The 1906 Act recommended the appointment of a full-time
director, and the first two holders of this post were Sir James Caw (1907–30) and
Sir Stanley Cursiter (1930–48).

Of course, the collection has been greatly and successfully expanded since
those early times and the growth of interest in art history has ensured that many
more visitors are now blessed with the 'liberal education' advocated by Croal
Thomson. As we celebrate the 150 years since the Gallery's foundation we also
look forward to the major development programme, the Playfair Project, which
will involve the establishment of the Royal Scottish Academy building as a major
international exhibitions centre. Plans are also underway to construct an
underground link between Playfair's two great buildings. This will house a
central concourse area, as well as a lecture theatre, an education suite, an
information technology hall and a restaurant for our visitors – all facilities sadly
lacking at present (fig.2). We trust that these sorely needed additional services
will enable us to provide the educational, intellectual and physical access to our
collections which twenty-first-century visitors, from Scotland and abroad, have
every right to expect and which we intend to deliver.

MICHAEL CLARKE
Keeper of the National Gallery of Scotland

Notes

ORDER OF GUIDE

The entries are divided into national schools within which the works are placed in approximate chronological order of execution.

MEASUREMENTS

Measurements are given in centimetres, height preceding width.

DATES

The date of a work is included at the top of the entry (on the artist / title line) only when it appears on the picture itself.

CONTRIBUTORS

Michael Clarke, Julia Lloyd Williams, Helen Smailes, Katrina Thomson, Aidan Weston-Lewis.

Bernardo Daddi c.1300–1348 · Triptych 1338

Daddi probably learned his trade in the Florentine workshop of Giotto (c.1270–1337), but was also influenced by painters of a more miniaturist tendency and by some of his Sienese contemporaries. He ran one of the most successful workshops in Florence in the first half of the fourteenth century, specialising in the production of relatively small-scale devotional paintings.

Dated 1338, this exquisitely crafted triptych, which incorporates precious metals and the most expensive pigments, would have been commissioned as an aid to prayer and meditation. It was probably kept for most of the year in a bedroom or study, although with the wings closed to protect the painted surface, it would have been easily portable and could have been taken on journeys. Alternatively, it may have adorned the altar of a small chapel belonging to a religious confraternity. The relegation of the *Virgin and Child with Saints* from the central panel to one of the wings is rare in Florentine art of this period, as is the inclusion in a triptych of this kind of scenes showing the martyrdom of St Peter (who was crucified upside-down) and *St Nicholas Donating the Dowries* (thereby allowing the daughters of an impoverished nobleman to marry). These unusual features no doubt reflect the wishes of the patron rather than spontaneous innovation on the part of the artist.

Centre
Crucifixion
Left wing
Nativity and Crucifixion of St Peter
Right wing
Virgin and Child Enthroned with Saints and St Nicholas Donating the Dowries
Tempera, silver (tarnished) and gold on panel, 89 × 83 (overall dimensions with wings open)
Purchased 1938
NG 1904

Vitale da Bologna before 1309–1359/61
The Adoration of the Kings with Saint Ursula and Saint Catherine of Alexandria

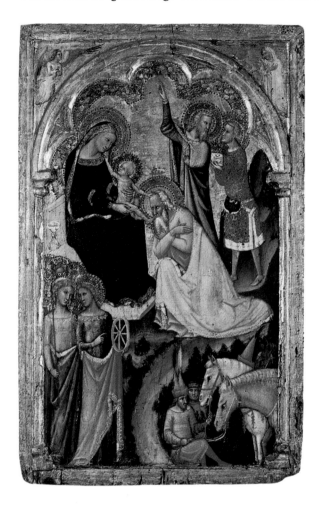

Tempera and gold on panel,
60.4 × 38.6
Purchased 1908
NG 952

Vitale was the first really distinctive artistic personality to emerge in Bologna, although his study of Giotto and of painters of the school of Rimini is reflected in his earlier work. He painted extensive fresco cycles as well as altarpieces and devotional panels. Vitale was active mainly in his native city and at Mezzaratta nearby, but he also carried out a few important commissions further afield (at Udine and Pomposa).

This panel originally formed the left portion of a diptych, the right panel of which, representing the *Pietà* (the body of Christ mourned by saints), is in the Fondazione Longhi, Florence. Hinged in the middle, the diptych would have been opened and closed like a book, to reveal or protect the sacred images painted on the inner surfaces. It has been dated to late in Vitale's career (c.1350–5) by comparison with an altarpiece of the *Coronation of the Virgin* in the church of San Salvatore, Bologna, which was commissioned in 1353. The expressive poses, gestures and glances which animate the scene, and the disparities in the relative scale of the figures, the horses and the setting (note the diminutive hedgerow and trees), are all characteristic of Vitale's highly idiosyncratic style. Christ's twisting, cross-legged pose, stabilised by the Virgin's long, tubular fingers, is particularly eye-catching. There are also touches of wit: one equerry is present only by virtue of his hat, while a glimpse of four haloes and a brow is enough to evoke St Ursula's eleven thousand martyred companions.

Lorenzo Monaco c.1370/75–c.1425 and Workshop
The Virgin and Child Enthroned

One of the foremost exponents of late
Gothic Florentine painting, the artist
was christened Piero di Giovanni, but
adopted the name Lorenzo when he
entered the Camaldolese monastery of
Santa Maria degli Angeli in 1391.
Stylistic evidence indicates that he may
have trained as a painter with Agnolo
Gaddi and as a manuscript illuminator
in the scriptorium of his own convent.
He also seems to have been closely
associated early in his career with the
important workshop of Jacopo and
Nardo di Cione.

This panel originally formed the
central component of a larger
altarpiece, the other elements of which
have not been convincingly identified.
The fragment of crimson drapery just
visible at the left edge must once have
belonged to a flanking saint. The
composition is a variation on the
central panel of Lorenzo's only
documented work, the *Monte Oliveto
Altarpiece* of 1407–10 (now in the
Accademia, Florence). The strange
form of the Virgin's seat, with its
lion's-head finials and cloven-hoof
feet, was probably intended as a
reference to King Solomon's 'Throne
of Wisdom'. The tooling and punch-
ing of the haloes and the textured
lining of the Virgin's cloak are
especially fine. The main contours of
this mantle were directly incised from
a template using a sharp instrument,
and the resulting indentations are still
visible on the surface. The painting
was probably largely executed by a
member of Lorenzo's studio, and has
been dated to about 1418.

Tempera and gold on panel,
101.6 × 61.7
Purchased 1965
NG 2271

Antonio Pisanello 1395 or before–1455

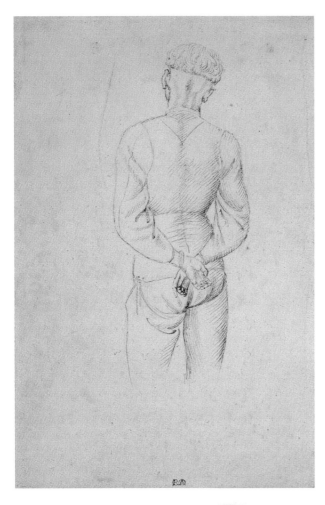

Study of a Young Man with his Hands tied behind his Back
Pen and brown ink over traces of metalpoint on cream paper, 26.8 × 18.6
David Laing Bequest to the Royal Scottish Academy, 1878; transferred to the National Gallery 1910
D 722

Gianfrancesco Gonzaga, 1st Marquis of Mantua
Cast bronze, 9.9 diameter
Purchased by the Patrons of the National Galleries of Scotland 1990
NG 2537

Probably born in Pisa (hence his name), Pisanello travelled extensively throughout Italy, but his main centres of activity were Verona and the Renaissance courts of Ferrara and Mantua. He was one of the most celebrated and multi-talented artists of his day, but many of his painted works have perished, and he is now best known for his drawings and medals.

This drawing was made in connection with a figure of a hanged man in the background of one of Pisanello's most famous works, a mural painting of *St George and the Princess* in the church of Sant'Anastasia, Verona (c.1433–8). The study was clearly drawn from a posed model, his taught right leg supporting his weight, whereas in the painting the body is suspended from a noose and both legs hang limp. Pisanello's spare ink lines capture the forms and textures with great skill and economy. So direct and unembellished a record of what the artist saw before him is exceptional among Italian drawings of this period.

Pisanello was the inventor of the modern portrait medal. He established a basic formula which was to remain standard for centuries, consisting of a profile portrait on one side, and on the other an image alluding, directly or cryptically, to the subject's virtues or accomplishments. This fine medal of Gianfrancesco Gonzaga (1395–1444) is a typical example. The Latin inscriptions on the front face (obverse) identify the sitter and allude to his military prowess. This theme is developed on the reverse (not illustrated), where the Marquis is shown mounted and wearing the armour appropriate to a professional military commander.

Francesco di Giorgio Martini 1439–1501

Borghesi was by profession a lawyer for the Sienese state, but this medal commemorates his role as commissioner general of the Sienese army at the battle of Poggio Imperiale in September 1479, when the Florentines were defeated by the combined forces of Pope Sixtus IV and King Ferdinand of Naples, supported by Siena. Borghesi was knighted by the commander of the Neapolitan forces, Alfonso, Duke of Calabria, and received the title of *Pater Patriae* from the Sienese government. Both honours are recorded in the inscription on the obverse of the medal. As a goddess of both wisdom and learning, and of war, the figure of Minerva on the reverse paid tribute to Borghesi's dual accomplishments. Notwithstanding the uneven patination of the obverse and minor casting flaws, this is an exceptionally fine example of the medal. Even areas vulnerable to wear, such as the delicate modelling of Minerva's clinging drapery, have remained sharp and legible.

A painter, miniaturist, sculptor, architect, military engineer, theorist and diplomat, Francesco di Giorgio was the most important artistic personality from Siena in the second half of the fifteenth century. He was active throughout Italy, especially later in his career, working in Urbino, Gubbio, Milan, Naples and Florence, as well as his native city. He probably took up medal-making after his move to the court of Federigo da Montefeltro in Urbino around 1476.

Obverse
*Borghese Borghesi
(1414–1490),
Jurisconsult of Siena*
Reverse
*Minerva with a Shield
and Lance*
Cast bronze, 6.3 diameter
Purchased 1989
NG 2502

Attributed to the Workshop of Andrea del Verrocchio c.1435–1488
The Virgin Adoring the Christ Child ('The Ruskin Madonna')

Tempera and oil(?) on canvas, transferred from panel, 106.7 × 76.3
Purchased with the aid of the National Art Collections Fund and the Pilgrim Trust 1975
NG 2338

The popular title of this painting records the fact that it was among the prized possessions of the nineteenth-century critic and artist John Ruskin. The painting is not in good condition, having been removed from its original wooden support and extensively restored. It nevertheless displays some remarkable features, notably the grandiose backdrop of classical architecture. The receding lines of the pavement follow a precise, geometric perspective grid incised into the gesso ground and still visible on the surface. The ruined architecture was probably meant to represent the Roman Temple of Peace, which according to legend collapsed at the moment of Christ's birth – a clear metaphor for the triumph of the new religion over the old. Christ's action of sucking a finger, as if he had pricked it and drawn blood, was presumably intended as a symbolic premonition of the Passion. This would explain the introspective, devotional attitude of the Virgin, who has just become aware of her son's momentous fate.

The authorship of the 'Ruskin Madonna' has been much debated. Traditionally ascribed to Filippo Lippi, most twentieth-century scholars favoured an attribution to the sculptor and painter Verrocchio, or to a member of his studio, largely on the basis of comparison with his sculpted reliefs (few undisputed paintings by him survive). More recently, the suggestion that the painting might be the work of the young Domenico Ghirlandaio (1448/9–1494), who went on to establish one of the most successful workshops in Florence, has gained some support.

Leonardo da Vinci 1452–1519
Studies of a Dog's Paw

The archetypal 'universal artist', Leonardo was a painter, sculptor, architect, engineer, inventor, writer, musician and natural scientist. Due to political vicissitudes, the demands and range of his projects, and his own perfectionism, very few of his undertakings were ever fully realised, although among these are two of the most famous works of art ever painted, the *Last Supper* (Santa Maria delle Grazie, Milan) and the *Mona Lisa* (Louvre, Paris). A pupil of Verrocchio in Florence, Leonardo divided most of his career between that city and Milan, although he later worked in Rome and finally for François I in France, where he died.

These studies of the left forepaw of a dog, viewed from different angles, are typical of Leonardo's analytical approach to the natural world. They were no doubt drawn from life, and the sheet may originally have formed part of a small notebook used for impromptu sketching. The technique, which allowed great precision but a restricted tonal range, involved drawing with a metal – usually silver – stylus on paper specially prepared with a coating of ground and tinted bonemeal. The drawing probably dates from the end of Leonardo's first Florentine period, about 1480. His later drawings of this type show a more rigorously scientific approach, and include annotated anatomical studies and drawings of dissections made in connection with a projected treatise on anatomy.

Recto and verso
Metalpoint on paper coated with a pale pink preparation, 14.1 × 10.7
Purchased by Private Treaty with the aid of the National Art Collections Fund 1991
D 5189

Sandro Botticelli 1444/5–1510 · The Virgin Adoring the Sleeping Christ Child

The creator of such celebrated works as the *Primavera* and *The Birth of Venus* (both in the Uffizi, Florence), Botticelli was one of the outstanding Florentine painters of the second half of the fifteenth century. He trained initially as a goldsmith, learned painting in the workshop of Filippo Lippi, and was an independent master by 1470. He received important commissions from various members of the powerful Medici family, and from others in their circle. His secular pictures, in particular, are imbued with the sophisticated humanist, literary culture of the Medici court. Botticelli's only notable absence from Florence was in the early 1480s, when he was summoned to Rome by Pope Sixtus IV to participate in the fresco decoration of the upper walls of the Sistine Chapel. In the 1490s he came under the sway of the influential Dominican reformist preacher, Fra Girolamo Savonarola, whose ideas are reflected in some of his later paintings.

The Virgin Adoring the Sleeping Christ Child was probably painted around 1490, but for whom is not known. Its compositional simplicity, elegant, gently swaying forms and great refinement of contour are characteristic features of Botticelli's later works. The basic design, with the Virgin in three-quarters view kneeling in adoration of the infant Christ, is derived from a compositional type invented by Botticelli's teacher Filippo Lippi, and was also used for the *Ruskin Madonna* (see page 18). The beautiful bower of thornless roses and the flower-filled meadow in the Edinburgh painting form an 'enclosed garden' (*hortus conclusus*), a symbol of the Virgin derived from imagery in the Old Testament Song of Solomon. Unusually for this period, and uniquely among Botticelli's many Madonna compositions, the artist shows the infant Christ asleep. Through the traditional association of sleep and death, this may have been intended as a premonition of his future self-sacrifice for mankind.

From a technical point of view, this picture is unusual in that it is painted on canvas, a support then only just coming into vogue in Italy and seldom employed by Botticelli (although it was used for *The Birth of Venus* and for one other important mythological painting by him). This, together with the lyrical, contemplative mood of the painting, may indicate that it was intended for a domestic setting in a palace or villa – in a study, bedroom or private oratory, perhaps – rather than for an altar in a church.

Tempera and gold on canvas, 122 × 80.5
Purchased with the aid of the Heritage Lottery Fund, the National Art Collections Fund, the Scottish Executive, the Bank of Scotland, the Royal Bank of Scotland, Sir Tom Farmer, the Dunard Fund, Mr and Mrs Kenneth Woodcock (donation made through the American Friends of the National Galleries of Scotland) and private donations 1999
NG 2709

Filippino Lippi 1457(?) – 1504 · *The Nativity with Two Angels*

Tempera, oil(?) and gold on panel, 25 × 37
Purchased 1931
NG 1758

Filippino was the illegitimate son of the painter and Carmelite friar Fra Filippo Lippi. After the latter's death in 1469, Filippino continued his training with Sandro Botticelli. Apart from periods of residence in Rome between 1488 and 1493, where he decorated a chapel in Santa Maria sopra Minerva, Filippino worked mainly in Florence, although he also supplied pictures for Prato (his home town), Lucca, Bologna, and Genoa.

This little panel probably once formed part of a predella – the horizontal zone at the base of an altarpiece which was often decorated with small-scale narratives – but it has not been related to a specific commission. The balletic poses and tousled hair of the angels are typical of Filippino, but their action of clutching the tails of the Virgin's mantle is unusual. The agitated, calligraphic application of highlights is paralleled in some of the artist's mature drawings. Although presumably intended to evoke the Holy Land, the turrets with steep conical roofs in the left background lend a distinctly northern European flavour, reflecting the pervasive influence of Netherlandish painted landscapes in Italy at this period.

Ferrarese School c.1470–80 · The Virgin and Child with Angels

As an exercise in *trompe l'œil* (eye-deceiving) illusionism, this arresting painting is unique in Italian art of the fifteenth century, but both its authorship and its intended meaning are unresolved. The viewer is led to believe that a prepared canvas or parchment attached by a tacking strip to a stretcher has been ruptured to reveal an image of the blessing Virgin Mary. The tattered remaining fragments of material and dislodged tacks seem to project forward from, and in one instance behind, the wooden stretcher, which doubles as a frame for the central image. A fly – a recurrent motif in illusionistic painting – is painted on one of the projecting shreds. It reinforces the theme of worldly transience introduced by the torn material, which contrasts with the monumental, stable, eternal image of the Virgin and Child behind. Adored by nimble angels with highly decorative – if hardly practical – wings, the Virgin is seated on a bridge before a panoramic landscape, which may allude to her role as intercessor between mortals and God. That the infant Jesus is shown asleep is a premonition of his future Passion, while the pomegranate held by the Virgin is a symbol of the Resurrection.

The artist responsible for this highly original work has not been identified. One ingenious recent proposal is that it may be by Gherardo d'Andrea Costa, who is documented as having supplied numerous works for the ruling D'Este family in Ferrara from 1457–71, but to whom no paintings can be securely attributed today.

Tempera, oil(?) and gold on panel, 58.5 × 44
Purchased 1921
NG 1535

Raphael 1483–1520

During a career which spanned barely twenty years, Raphael (Raffaello Santi) rose from modest beginnings to the summit of his profession and exerted a more enduring influence on the course of European painting than any other single artist. He trained first with his father, Giovanni Santi, and later with Pietro Perugino. Early in his career he was active in his native Urbino, southern Tuscany and Perugia. He was based in Florence from about 1504 until he was summoned to Rome by Pope Julius II in 1508 to decorate the papal apartments (Stanze) in the Vatican, a project which continued under Leo X. Other important Roman commissions included designs for a series of tapestries for the walls of the Sistine Chapel, major altarpieces, frescoes in the Villa Farnesina and in the Vatican Loggie, portraits, and various architectural projects (he was appointed architect to St Peter's, Rome in 1514). He ran a busy workshop and came increasingly to rely on the help of assistants.

Despite their very different appearance, *The Holy Family with a Palm Tree* and *The Bridgewater Madonna* were probably painted within a year or two of each other (c.1506–8). They belong to a highly inventive and varied sequence of Madonna compositions dating from Raphael's Florentine period, characterised above all by a sense of harmonious balance, grace and intimacy. The circular (tondo) format of *The Holy Family with a Palm Tree* was especially popular in Florence, and Raphael

The Holy Family with a Palm Tree
Oil and gold on canvas, transferred from panel, 101.5 diameter
Lent by the Duke of Sutherland 1945

arranged his figures so as to emphasise this shape, with the centrally placed Christ Child acting as the hub. Both the composition and the luminous palette were strongly influenced by the early work of Raphael's friend Fra Bartolomeo. Dressed in rich gold and midnight blue, Joseph is accorded unusual prominence as he offers the infant Jesus a handful of flowers. The veil which so enchantingly bonds mother and child in a figure-of-eight may allude prophetically to the winding-cloth in which Christ was to be entombed. The palm tree, abundant flowers, paling fence, and what may be a sealed fountain or well-head, all recall imagery found in special devotions (litanies) to the Virgin Mary, derived in part from the Old Testament Song of Solomon.

The elegantly curving, *contrapposto* pose of the Virgin in *The Bridgewater Madonna* reflects Raphael's intensive study of Leonardo da Vinci. The composition is supremely poised. A sense of urgency generated by Christ's intense gaze and energetically twisting body is neutralised by his mother's tender expression and protective embrace. The idea may have been that Christ has just experienced an intimation of his momentous fate. Although the figure group was carefully worked out in a series of preparatory drawings, the setting was finalised only at a late stage. Technical analysis has revealed that Raphael initially painted a full landscape background, then reduced this to a view through an arched window, and finally painted it out altogether – presumably to focus the viewer's attention on the figure group.

The so-called *Madonna del Passeggio* is not strictly speaking a Madonna

composition at all, for it represents the legendary meeting of the young St John the Baptist with the Holy Family on their return from exile in Egypt. The picture is exceptionally well preserved, having escaped the transfer from panel to canvas suffered by the other two Sutherland Raphaels in the eighteenth century. Although it no doubt left Raphael's studio as a work by the master and was admired for centuries as such, *The Madonna del Passeggio* in fact appears to have been painted entirely by a talented assistant, possibly Gianfrancesco Penni (1496– after 1528). It is even doubtful whether

The Virgin and Child ('The Bridgewater Madonna')
Oil and gold on canvas, transferred from panel,
82 × 57
Lent by the Duke of Sutherland 1945

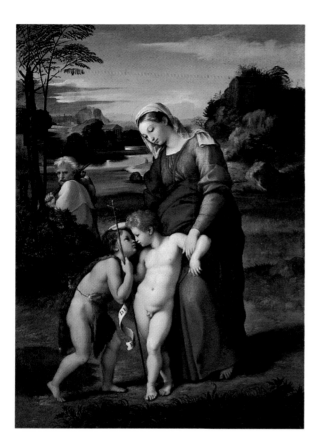

Raphael was closely involved in its design, for the chunky physiques and rather mannered poses of the infants would be untypical of him. The landscape, especially the rocky outcrop at the right, is stylistically the most distinctive part of the picture.

A consummate draughtsman, Raphael's beautiful life study of a *Kneeling Nude Woman with her Left Arm Raised* was made in connection with a composition of the *Toilet of Psyche* destined for a lunette in the entrance loggia of the Villa Chigi (now the Farnesina) in Rome, but never carried out. A drawn copy from the late sixteenth century records the whole composition. The frescoes on the ceiling of the loggia, illustrating other episodes from the fable of Psyche, were painted around 1518 by Raphael's assistants, principally Giulio Romano and Giovanni da Udine. Only some of the surviving preparatory studies for the loggia are by Raphael himself, but he undoubtedly retained overall control of the project. The patron was Agostino Chigi, the extremely wealthy papal banker with whom Raphael was on intimate terms.

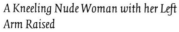

The Madonna del Passeggio
Oil and gold on panel, 90 × 63
Lent by the Duke of Sutherland 1945

A Kneeling Nude Woman with her Left Arm Raised
Red chalk, with touches of black chalk, over stylus underdrawing on off-white paper, 27.9 × 18.7
Purchased by Private Treaty with the aid of the National Heritage Memorial Fund, the National Art Collections Fund and the Pilgrim Trust 1987
D 5145

Giulio Romano c.1499–1546
The Holy Family with the Infant St John the Baptist ('The Novar Madonna')

A prodigious talent, Giulio probably joined Raphael's workshop around 1515 and within two years he was being entrusted with the execution of major projects. With Gianfrancesco Penni, he assumed joint control of Raphael's studio after his death in 1520. In 1524 he entered the service of Federico II Gonzaga, Duke of Mantua, as court painter, architect and designer, and he remained in Mantua for the rest of his life. Giulio Romano was one of the leading exponents of the Mannerist style in Italy. His masterpiece is the Palazzo Te in Mantua, which he both designed and decorated.

This *Holy Family* is one of a series of paintings dating from the years around 1520 in which Giulio reworked compositions by Raphael in his own idiom. The figure group is derived from a Raphael composition known as the *Madonna of the Rose* (Prado, Madrid). Giulio elected to show more of the Virgin's legs, only to cut them off abruptly at the ankles. He intro-duced a nocturnal, outdoor setting with an imposing rusticated archway in the background, within which the figure of Joseph holding a lamp and leading a donkey can just be glimpsed (in Raphael's composition he is integrated into the main figure group). Although freely painted, Giulio's picture surface is harder and more polished than Raphael's, the colours are more acidic and their contrasts more strident. The effect of these changes – which are entirely character-istic of Giulio – was to transform an intimate and balanced composition into a more spacious but more unstable and discordant one.

Oil and gold on panel, 82.5 × 63.5
Purchased with the aid of a National Heritage
Purchase Grant (Scotland) 1980
NG 2398

Andrea del Sarto 1486–1530
Domenico di Jacopo Becuccio, called 'Becuccio Bicchieraio'

Oil on panel, 86 × 67
Purchased 1967
NG 2297

The sitter was a glass-maker (*bicchieraio*), which explains the prominent inclusion of a glass jug and dish in the portrait. According to the artists' biographer Vasari, Becuccio was a very close friend of Del Sarto, and he commissioned an important altarpiece from him for his home village of Gambassi (now in the Palazzo Pitti, Florence). Comparison with a portrait roundel of Becuccio (now in the Art Institute of Chicago), which was originally inserted in the predella of this altarpiece, confirms beyond doubt the identity of the sitter in the Edinburgh portrait. It was previously considered to be a self-portrait by Del Sarto. The quiet, reflective mood of the portrait is emphasised by the muted palette of black, greys and greens, enlivened only by the pale yellow and orange of the citrus fruit. Numerous adjustments to the contours are faintly visible as *pentimenti* in the background around the figure.

Andrea del Sarto was the leading Florentine painter of the early sixteenth century, whom Vasari described as 'the painter without flaws'. He trained under Piero di Cosimo and was an independent master by 1508. He specialised in the production of altarpieces and other religious works, but also painted important frescoes and a few portraits. With the exception of a year (1518–19) spent in France at the court of François I, he worked almost exclusively in his native Florence.

Francesco Ubertini, called Bacchiacca 1494–1557
Moses Striking the Rock

The artists' biographer Vasari describes how Bacchiacca contributed scenes from the Old Testament, principally from the story of Moses, to decorate a temporary structure commissioned by a Florentine guild of jug-makers (or jug-vendors) for a festival held in 1525. As elaborate jugs appear everywhere in the Edinburgh painting, this has led to the credible suggestion that it may be a spin-off from that commission. With its broad spectrum of facial types, vibrantly coloured costumes, elaborate headdresses, finely crafted vessels and jewellery, and accompanying menagerie of exotic birds and beasts, the painting amounts to a conspicuous and self-conscious display of the artist's skill. It mattered little, it seems, that such opulence was inappropriate to the biblical tale, which relates how Moses miraculously conjured water from a rock to slake the thirst of the children of Israel on their journey to the Promised Land.

Bacchiacca was born in Florence, where he trained in the studio of Perugino and had close links with Andrea del Sarto and Franciabigio. Although innovative in his use of colour, he was in most respects a conservative and eclectic painter, often adapting figures from other artists' work, especially from prints. He specialised in the production of cabinet paintings for domestic settings. The Edinburgh panel illustrates well Bacchiacca's talents as a painter of small-scale figure compositions and of animals, which were singled out by Vasari as his principal strengths.

Oil and gold on panel,
100 × 80
Purchased 1967
NG 2291

Lorenzo Lotto c.1480–1556/7 · The Virgin and Child with Saints Jerome, Peter, Francis and an Unidentified Female Saint

Oil on canvas, transferred from panel, 82.5 × 105
Purchased by Private Treaty with the aid of the National Heritage Memorial Fund 1984
NG 2418

Lotto was born in Venice and probably trained there in the workshop of Giovanni Bellini. Although he received some important commissions in Venice, he spent much of his career working in more provincial centres, notably at Treviso, Bergamo and in various towns in the Marche. Altarpieces, smaller devotional paintings and portraits formed the mainstay of his production. Lotto seems to have been a rather difficult and restless character, beset by periods of financial hardship and bouts of melancholy. His highly personal and idiosyncratic style found no real followers.

One of Lotto's earliest surviving works, datable to about 1505, this picture owes a clear stylistic and compositional debt to Bellini.

However, some slightly eccentric features are already apparent, such as the curtain which bisects the composition (and the Virgin's head) horizontally, the crisp, angular draperies, and the large hands and highly individualised features of the protagonists. The Christ Child reads a scroll presented to him by St Jerome which is signed LOTVS, the latinised form of the artist's name. St Francis, at the right, appears to intercede with the Virgin on behalf of the viewer, suggesting that whoever commissioned the picture may have been particularly devoted to that saint. The woodcutters felling a tree in the background allude symbolically to the wood of the cross and therefore to Christ's Passion.

Giovanni Cariani c.1485–after 1547 · *Portrait of a Young Woman as Saint Agatha*

Born into a family of minor nobility in the Val Brembana near Bergamo, Cariani is first recorded as a painter in Venice in 1509, and he was based there for most of his career. He may have trained in the workshop of Giovanni Bellini, and was much influenced by the novel style introduced by Giorgione and developed by Titian, Sebastiano del Piombo and Palma Vecchio. Many of his best pictures date from 1517–23, when he was resident in Bergamo.

St Agatha was an early Christian virgin martyr from Catania in Sicily. Her great beauty won her many admirers, but she had taken a vow of chastity. Among her frustrated suitors was the Roman governor, whose vain attempt to torture her into submission culminated in having her breasts cut off. The highly individualised features of the young woman in Cariani's painting and her expensive contemporary costume suggest that this is a portrait of a young woman in the guise of her name-saint. This interpretation is supported by the adoption of several compositional conventions of contemporary Venetian portraiture, such as the foreground parapet with its fictive relief, and the view through the arch into a landscape. The intended message is highly ambiguous, for while the young woman is presented in the guise of a virgin martyr, her expression and gestures are sensuous and seductive. The placement of the palm stem between the severed breasts – one of which she fingers gently – was no accident, and this suggestiveness is emphasised by the otherwise inexplicable positioning of her left hand.

Oil on canvas,
69 × 58
Purchased 1989
NG 2494

Titian c.1485/90–1576

The Three Ages of Man
Oil on canvas, 90 × 150.7
Lent by the Duke of
Sutherland 1945

Titian (Tiziano Vecellio) was the most celebrated painter of the Venetian school during his lifetime, and has retained that distinction ever since. He was born at an unknown date in Pieve di Cadore in the Dolomites, but came to Venice as a boy and was based there throughout his long career. He probably trained in the workshop of Gentile and Giovanni Bellini, and was later closely associated with Giorgione. His earliest securely datable works are some frescoes of 1511 in Padua. Titian excelled as a painter of altarpieces, devotional works, classical mythology and allegory, and his unrivalled talents as a portraitist were in huge demand. He received prestigious commissions from Venetian churches and the Venetian state, and numbered among his most important patrons the courts of Ferrara, Mantua and Urbino; Pope Paul III; the Holy Roman Emperor Charles V (who knighted him in

1533); and his son Philip II of Spain, the recipient of many of his best pictures from the 1550s onwards. Titian's work is prized above all for its sumptuous colour and lively brush-work, which became increasingly broken and impressionistic as he grew older.

The Three Ages of Man, an early work painted around 1512–14, is a poetic meditation on the transience of human life and love set in an idyllic pastoral landscape. At the right, two sleeping infants, blissfully unaware of the affairs of the heart, are clambered over by the mischievous winged Cupid, god of love. The young lovers at the left, their passions inflamed by a duet on the flute, stare ardently into one another's eyes as they move to embrace. The old man in the middle distance, looking very much like a penitent St Jerome, contemplates two skulls – by implication those of two former lovers. This note of melan-choly is offset by the inclusion of a church behind, with its promise of eternal salvation. Although placed in a unified landscape, each figure group is arranged into a self-contained pyramid, which encourages the spectator to view them as separate episodes. The painting echoes themes found in ancient and contemporary pastoral poetry, but it does not seem to illustrate a specific story.

The bright palette of *The Three Ages of Man* was further intensified in *The Virgin and Child with St John the Baptist and an Unidentified Saint*, which probably dates from a few years later. Although traditionally described as a Holy Family, the identification of the bearded saint in purple and red as Joseph is far from certain. St John, who recalls the young man in *The Three Ages of Man*, points towards the lamb in allusion to his famous description of Jesus as the sacrificial 'Lamb of God'. Titian here lavished particular attention on naturalistic details and the contrasting textures of flesh, foliage, bark, fleece and draperies.

According to legend, Venus was born of the sea fully grown from the foam produced by the genitals of the castrated Uranus. Titian shows the beautiful goddess striding through the shallows, wringing her hair, having floated ashore in the diminutive scallop shell included at the left. In painting *Venus Rising from the Sea*, Titian would have been well aware that he was inviting comparison with the most celebrated painter of antiquity, Apelles, who had made the subject famous. Dating from about 1520–25, his picture is a subtle harmony of pastel blues and pinks, set off against the vibrant reddish-gold of Venus's hair.

The Virgin and Child with St John the Baptist and an Unidentified Saint
Oil on canvas, transferred from panel, 62.7 × 93
Lent by the Duke of Sutherland 1945

Venus Rising from the Sea ('Venus Anadyomene')
Oil on canvas, 74 × 56.2 · Lent by the Duke of Sutherland 1945

Diana and Actaeon
*Oil on canvas, 188 × 204.5
Lent by the Duke of
Sutherland 1945*

In contrast to the three earlier
paintings by Titian, the *Diana and
Actaeon* and *Diana and Callisto* are well
documented. They are among his
most acclaimed works, and originally formed part of a series of seven
mythological paintings ('*poesie*'),
with subjects drawn mainly from
Ovid's *Metamorphoses*, which Titian
painted for Philip II of Spain. In June
1559 the artist reported to his patron
that the two Diana scenes were
finished (although he in fact
continued to work on them until
September), specifying that they had

been begun three years previously.
Closely related both visually and
thematically, they were conceived as a
pair within the larger series, which
was developed and extended on a
piecemeal basis.

In *Diana and Actaeon*, the hunter
Actaeon unwittingly enters the secret
glade where Diana and her nymphs
are bathing. Outraged at his intrusion,
the goddess transformed him into
stag, to be torn apart by his own
hunting dogs. The stag's skull
surmounting the pillar alludes to
Actaeon's grisly fate.

Diana and Callisto
Oil on canvas, 187 × 204.5
Lent by the Duke of Sutherland 1945

In the pendant painting, the
unfortunate nymph Callisto, who had
been seduced by Jupiter, was stripped
by her companions at the command
of the chaste moon-goddess Diana to
reveal her pregnancy. Banished for
her shameful state, Callisto was
transformed into a bear by Jupiter's
jealous wife Juno, but was later
immortalised by him as the constella-
tion of the Great Bear.

Jacopo Bassano c.1510–1592 · The Adoration of the Kings

Oil on canvas, 183 × 235
Purchased by the Royal
Scottish Academy, 1856;
transferred to the National
Gallery 1910
NG 100

Jacopo Bassano (or dal Ponte) was the outstanding talent among a family of painters spanning three generations from the town of Bassano del Grappa on the Venetian mainland. He trained initially with his father, and then, in the 1530s, with Bonifazio de' Pitati in Venice. From about 1540 he lived permanently in Bassano del Grappa and directed the family workshop, although he remained receptive to artistic developments in Venice and elsewhere. Four of Jacopo's sons became painters, with whom he frequently collaborated. Altarpieces and other religious works formed the mainstay of his production. Later in his career these often incorporated significant pastoral or genre elements.

The Adoration of the Kings is probably identical with the picture of this subject painted in 1542 for one Jacomo Gisi, according to an entry in the account book of the Bassano workshop. The features of the king at the centre in green and gold stripes may be those of the patron, and the boys behind him also appear to be portraits, presumably of his sons. Vibrant in colour and full of movement and incidental detail, the painting shows Bassano at his most inventive, having fully integrated the lessons of Titian, Pordenone, and his teacher Bonifazio. The compellingly convincing portrayal of the animals, columbine plant, tree-stump, and apple tree lends a note of rustic naturalism to the scene. The ruined architecture, on the other hand, is partly adapted from a woodcut by Albrecht Dürer.

Jacopo Tintoretto 1518–1594 · *Christ Carried to the Tomb*

Jacopo Robusti was nicknamed Tintoretto from his father's trade of dyer (*tintore*). He worked almost exclusively in Venice, his native city, where he may have been taught by Titian. In typical Venetian fashion, his highly productive workshop was a family business where two of his sons and a daughter were trained. Among his most celebrated works is the extensive cycle of religious canvases in the Scuola di San Rocco.

This painting was commissioned around 1555–60 by two brothers of the Dal Basso family for the altar of their newly-constructed chapel in the Venetian church of San Francesco della Vigna. We know from reproductive prints that it was originally arched in format, with a flying angel holding a crown of thorns at the top, but it was cut out of its frame, possibly by thieves, at some time in the early seventeenth century, leaving most of the angel behind (its feet are just visible at the top of the Edinburgh canvas). The composition is arranged into two distinct tiers, with the principal scene of Christ borne to the tomb by torchlight – his body elongated out of all proportion – separated from the more prominent foreground group of the three Maries, where the Virgin swoons from inconsolable grief. The bold, highly visible brushstrokes, strong local colours and figures charged with energy and movement are all hallmarks of Tintoretto's style.

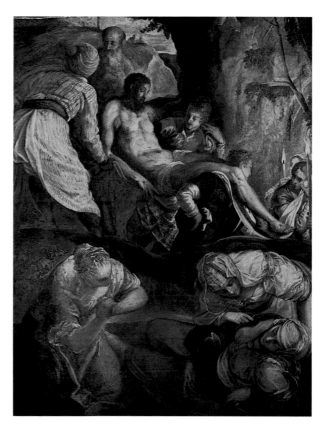

Oil on canvas, 164 × 127.5 (cut down)
Purchased by Private Treaty with the aid of the National Heritage Memorial Fund 1984
NG 2419

Oil on canvas, 97 × 141
Purchased by the Royal
Institution, 1830;
transferred to the National
Gallery 1859
NG 10

The two younger women are almost certainly courtesans, while the darker-skinned woman at the left is presumably their procuress. There is a poignant contrast between the young woman at the right, who modestly attempts to cover her nakedness, and her companion, who unashamedly bares all for the viewer's inspection. Mildly erotic subject-matter of this type had been popularised in Venice by Titian and Palma Vecchio during the 1510s. In Bordon's painting it is enriched through allusions to other themes. The inclusion of a comb and mirror evokes both the mythological subject of the toilet of Venus and the allegorical *vanitas* theme of the transience of physical beauty. The prominently placed ointment jar may have been intended as a reference to the reformed and penitent biblical courtesan Mary Magdalen, whose

principal attribute it is. Probably painted in the mid-1540s, the bulky figures, elaborate hairstyles, fussily folded and patterned draperies and precisely detailed architecture are all typical of Bordon's mature style.

Born at Treviso on the Venetian mainland, Bordon is recorded as a painter in Venice in 1518, where he may have trained under Titian, and was active principally in these two centres. He was one of the Venetian painters most influenced by the elaborate and artificial Mannerist style imported from central Italy.

Paolo Veronese 1528–1588 · Mars, Venus and Cupid

Paolo Caliari trained in Verona under Antonio Badile, and was an independent master by 1544. Having enjoyed some early success, by 1555 he had moved definitively to Venice, where he was known as 'Veronese' after his birthplace. Assisted by his brother and later by his sons, his studio became one of the busiest in Venice and, in terms of sheer output, the only serious competitor to the Tintoretto workshop. A superb colourist, Veronese is best remembered as a painter of altarpieces, religious narratives and decorative mythologies teeming with figures, fine fabrics and incidental detail.

In this late work of about 1580, Venus gently comforts her son Cupid, who has been frightened by a lively little spaniel – a whimsical intrusion of an everyday incident into a mythological subject. The goddess of love is somewhat awkwardly seated on Mars' knee. The figure of Mars may have been inserted (possibly by an assistant) at a relatively late stage in the evolution of the composition, since he does not feature in Veronese's sheet of preparatory sketches now in the British Museum. The tonal imbalance of the painting (certainly more pronounced now than it was originally) is due to a technical peculiarity, the figures of Venus and Cupid alone having been prepared with a thick layer of white underpaint, which guaranteed the luminosity of their flesh. The very sketchy treatment of Cupid's wings indicates that the painting may have been left unfinished.

Oil on canvas,
165.2 × 126.5
Purchased by the Royal
Institution, 1859;
transferred to the National
Gallery 1867
NG 339

Giovanni Battista Moroni c.1522–1578
Portrait of Giovanni Bressani (1490–1560)

Oil on canvas, 114.2 × 81
Purchased by Private Treaty
1977
NG 2347

This portrait is signed and dated 1562, but none of the inscriptions specifies the identity of the sitter. That it indeed portrays Bressani can be established by comparison with a medal and another painted portrait of him, and that it is posthumous explains why one inscription tells us that Moroni had 'painted him whom he did not see'. Bressani was one of the leading literary figures in sixteenth-century Bergamo, a prolific composer of Latin and vernacular verse, epitaphs, and prose. It is to his talents in this field that the splendid still-life elements in the portrait refer, among them two sheets of (illegible) poetry, an ink-well in the shape of a foot, and a pounce-pot for sprinkling sand over wet ink in order to dry it. The inscription at the bottom of the page nearest the viewer reads: 'This painting represents well the image of my body, but that of my spirit is provided by my many writings.' The placement of the sitter's chair at right-angles to the viewer was an arrangement used by Moroni for several other portraits.

Born at Albino near Bergamo, Moroni was a pupil of Moretto in Brescia, although he was subsequently mainly active in Bergamo. He painted some accomplished religious works, but is rightly best known today for his exceptional skills as a portraitist. His portraits are distinguished by their pronounced naturalism and inventive repertoire of poses and settings.

Domenichino 1581–1641
The Adoration of the Shepherds

Domenichino was born in Bologna and trained there under Denys Calvaert and then in the Carracci Academy. In 1602 he moved to Rome and became a favoured assistant to Annibale Carracci. He was the leading exponent of the more restrained, classical tendency in Italian painting of the earlier seventeenth century, characterised by ordered, easily legible compositions and clearly articulated gestures and expressions. He enjoyed considerable success in Rome and Bologna before moving to Naples in 1631.

This painting was described by the usually reliable artists' biographer Bellori (1672) as a copy by Domenichino after a lost picture by his master, Annibale Carracci, in whose studio he was working at the time it was painted. However, surviving evidence indicates that Domenichino's point of departure was in reality a group of drawings by Annibale (and one by his brother Agostino), rather than a painting. Ideas copied and adapted from these, together with original life studies of his own, were fused together to form the present composition. As Bellori noted, the dramatic illumination, with the entire scene bathed in brilliant divine light emanating from the infant Christ in the centre, is derived ultimately from an altarpiece by Correggio known as *La Notte* (now the Gemäldegalerie, Dresden). Given this multiplicity of sources, Domenichino's composition is remarkable for its structural coherence and clarity.

Oil on canvas, 143 × 115
Purchased 1971
NG 2313

Guido Reni 1575–1642

Guido Reni was probably the most successful and sought-after Italian painter of the first half of the seventeenth century, despite being notoriously difficult and temperamental. Like Domenichino, he trained in his native Bologna first with Calvaert and then in the Carracci Academy. He established his reputation in Rome, where he was resident from 1601 to 1614, and thereafter was based mainly in Bologna, executing commissions for the most elevated patrons in Italy and abroad. His paintings display an unfailing sense of grace and elegance combined with a powerful naturalism in the depiction of forms and textures.

The Gallery owns a fine group of drawings by Reni, but only one painting, dating from the very end of his career. *The Fall of Phaeton*, which is a preparatory study for Reni's ceiling fresco in the former Palazzo Zani in Bologna, is one of his most impressive early sheets, dating from before his departure for Rome. According to Ovid's *Metamorphoses*, the sun god Apollo rashly allowed his son Phaeton to drive his chariot across the skies. The inexperienced Phaeton soon lost control and to avoid catastrophe was sent hurtling to earth by one of Jupiter's thunderbolts. Reni all but eliminated the chariot and arranged Phaeton and the horses into a rhythmically swirling centralised pattern, ideally suited to a square ceiling.

Drawn in Reni's customary feathery chalk technique, the life-study of a muscular torso and club-wielding arm is preparatory for a painting of *Hercules Slaying the Hydra* (Louvre, Paris). This is part of a series of four canvases illustrating feats of Hercules painted for the Duke of Mantua around 1620, which are among the artist's most celebrated mythological works.

The Fall of Phaeton
Pen and brown ink and wash over black chalk, on off-white paper; 37.5 × 32.5
Purchased 1974
D 5011

Study of a Male Torso
Black and red chalk, heightened with white, on grey paper; 25.2 × 35.9
David Laing Bequest to the Royal Scottish Academy; transferred to the National Gallery 1910
D 711

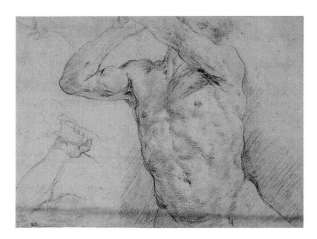

Towards the end of his life Reni produced a group of canvases using a restricted palette of mainly pastel shades and a sketchy, seemingly unfinished technique, of which *Moses with Pharaoh's Crown* is an excellent example. It was probably among the paintings left in the artist's studio at the time of his death. Although he may have intended to work up some details further, the overall descriptive economy and lack of finish seems to have been intentional. Reni here supplied so little information that there is even some doubt as to the subject of the painting, but it probably shows the infant Moses holding Pharaoh's crown just prior to trampling on it as a symbolic rejection of Pharaoh's rule over the exiled Israelites.

Moses with Pharaoh's Crown
Oil on canvas, 132.2 × 172.7
Purchased 1979
NG 2375

Guercino 1591–1666

The Virgin and Child with the Infant St John the Baptist

Oil on canvas, 86.5 × 110
Purchased by the Royal Institution, 1830; transferred to the National Gallery 1859
NG 40

Giovanni Francesco Barbieri was nicknamed Guercino on account of his squint. He was born in the town of Cento near Bologna and, with the exception of two years spent in Rome (1621–3), he lived there until 1642, when he moved his studio to Bologna following the death of his rival Guido Reni. He was largely self-taught, developing a highly original, naturalistic manner of painting, which he modified following his visit to Rome in order to conform to the more classical tastes then in vogue.

These two pictures, painted some thirty-five years apart, illustrate well the profound transformation Guercino's style underwent over the course of his career. In *The Virgin and Child with the Infant St John*, which dates from about 1615, the erratic, heavily contrasted light effects, saturated colours, unidealised models (notably the dumpy little figure of the Baptist), and the bold foreshortening of the Virgin's left hand are all typical of

Guercino's early style. The pose of the Christ Child asleep on a white cloth deliberately evokes representations of Christ's body in a pietà or a lamentation. In a charming detail, the Virgin uses her little finger to help the Baptist read the motto 'Ecce Agnus Dei' ('Behold the Lamb of God') inscribed on his scroll.

Erminia Finding the Wounded Tancred illustrates a scene from Torquato Tasso's great epic poem about the Crusades, *Gerusalemme Liberata* (1581). Alerted to Tancred's plight by his squire Vafrino, the tearful Erminia rushes with outstretched arms towards her injured lover, her streaming hair and agitated draperies reflecting her inner turmoil. The poignant emotion and drama of an instant is captured and frozen in time. Compared to Guercino's earlier painting, the composition is more balanced, the forms more legible, the colours paler and the lighting more even. The sombre hues of the land-

Erminia Finding the Wounded Tancred
Oil on canvas, 244 × 287
Purchased by Private Treaty with the aid of the
Heritage Lottery Fund, the National Art
Collections Fund and corporate and private
donations 1996
NG 2656

scape enhance the gravity of the event.
The picture was commissioned in 1650
by the Papal Legate of Bologna,
Cardinal Fabrizio Savelli, as a companion to an Erminia and the Shepherd he
had bought from Guercino the
previous year, but before it was
completed he agreed to cede it to the
Duke and Duchess of Mantua, who
paid for it in May 1652.

Orazio Borgianni c.1578–1616 · Saint Christopher Carrying the Infant Christ

Oil on canvas, 104 × 78
Presented to the Royal Scottish Academy by Sir
John Watson Gordon PRSA, 1850; transferred
to the National Gallery 1910
NG 48

Borgianni was Tuscan by birth but moved to Rome as a boy. His first dated work (1593) was painted for a church in Sicily. He probably travelled to Spain some time in the late 1590s and is documented there in 1603 and 1605. By 1606 he was back in Rome, where he seems to have been based for the remainder of his life. His fluent handling of paint was influenced by sixteenth-century Venetian and Lombard artists, and he was much impressed by the mature works of Caravaggio.

This picture is one of several surviving versions of this composition by Borgianni, who frequently produced two or more variants of successful compositions. It was also reproduced in an etching by him. The largest – but not necessarily the earliest – painted version was discovered recently in a church near Seville. The nocturnal setting and the poses of the figures are based on a painting by the German artist Adam Elsheimer, but the dramatic realism – especially the domination of the foreground by the saint's massive left leg – is derived from Caravaggio. According to legend, St Christopher carried a child across a river on his shoulders, but with each step his passenger became heavier and heavier. On reaching the bank, the child revealed himself as Christ and explained that Christopher had been carrying the weight of the world upon his shoulders.

Giulio Cesare Procaccini 1574–1625 · *The Raising of the Cross*

Born in Bologna, Procaccini moved with his family to Milan as a boy, where he learned painting from his father and elder brothers. Having been active initially as a sculptor, he turned to painting around 1600 and became one of the leading Milanese painters of the first quarter of the seventeenth century. Later in his career he also worked in Genoa, where his style was influenced by Rubens's paintings, and for the court of Savoy in Turin. Procaccini's style, which was strongly rooted in the sixteenth-century Milanese tradition, shows little in the way of consistent development over the course of his career.

The Raising of the Cross combines passages of gruesome realism with a highly contrived, densely packed composition full of energy, emotion and flashes of brilliant colour. These qualities are typical not only of Procaccini's own mature works, but of the late Mannerist style in Lombardy more generally. The design hinges on the dramatically receding diagonal of Christ's tortured body on the cross. *The Raising of the Cross* has been associated with three other scenes from the Passion of Christ by Procaccini of similar dimensions and style, and there may once have been more, but the original location of this hypothetical ensemble is not known. All the canvases in the series appear to date from 1615 to 1620.

Oil on canvas, 218 × 148.6
Purchased 1965
NG 2276

Gianlorenzo Bernini 1598–1680 · Portrait Bust of Monsignor Carlo Antonio dal Pozzo, Archbishop of Pisa (1547–1607)

First and foremost a sculptor, Bernini was also an architect, urban planner, painter, and designer of decorative arts and temporary structures for festivals, funerals and the theatre. A prodigious talent, he learned to carve from his father, Pietro. His early portrait busts and mythological groups already show a technical sophistication and a command of the human form in motion rivalled only by the greatest sculptors of antiquity. Over sixty years Bernini's skills were harnessed by a succession of eight popes in the service of the Catholic Church and the promotion of their families. He did more than any other single artist to shape the appearance of Rome as we see it today.

This bust was carved around 1622–4 for the sitter's nephew, Cassiano dal Pozzo, a scholar, antiquarian, collector and one of the leading figures in the cultural life of Rome, who is best known to art historians as an important patron of Poussin. The portrait is a touching posthumous tribute to the archbishop, who had been Cassiano's mentor and had paid for his education, and it was displayed in a prominent position in his Roman palace. The arresting power and vitality of the bust are all the more remarkable given that Bernini never saw the sitter (who had died some fifteen years before it was carved) and probably based his likeness on painted portraits and possibly a death mask.

Marble, 82 × 70 (maximum dimensions, including integral socle) Purchased by Private Treaty with the aid of the National Heritage Memorial Fund, the National Art Collections Fund, the Pilgrim Trust, the J. Paul Getty Jr Charitable Trust and private donations 1986
NG 2436

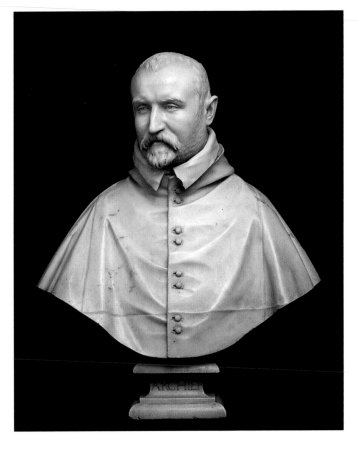

Giovanni Battista Gaulli, called Baciccio 1639–1709
Portrait of Gianlorenzo Bernini (1598–1680)

This sympathetic and penetrating portrayal of the elderly Bernini was painted around 1675 and is almost certainly one of the five portraits of him that appear, without attributions, in his post-mortem inventory. Its vibrant brushwork and bold touches of impasto establish it as the prime version of a portrait known in numerous variants and copies. The sitter's obvious signs of ageing are offset by his alert gaze and the 'speaking gesture' of his hand emerging from the folds of his cloak. This appealing image of a brilliant but difficult man with numerous detractors seems to have been deliberately employed by his heirs to help foster a positive posthumous reputation. It was the model for the engraved frontispiece to Filippo Baldinucci's flattering and polemical biography of Bernini (1682), and it was also the prototype for the official portrait of Bernini commissioned later for the Roman Academy of St Luke.

Baciccio was one of the foremost exponents of High Baroque decorative painting in Rome, but it was his talents as a portraitist that first established his reputation. Genoese by birth and training, he moved to Rome around 1658 and by the mid-1660s he was on close terms with Bernini, who did much to foster his career. It is especially fitting that Baciccio should, in turn, have been so directly involved in the perpetuation of his master's memory.

Oil on canvas, 99 × 74.5
Purchased with the aid of the National Art Collections Fund 1998
NG 2694

Sebastiano Ricci 1659–1734
Christ Healing the Blind Man

Oil on canvas, 52 × 67.5
Purchased with the aid of
the National Art Collections
Fund 1994
NG 2623

Sebastiano Ricci was one of the most successful Venetian artists of his generation, and was a key figure in the transition of Italian painting from full-blown Baroque to elegant and airy Rococo. After training in Venice he went to Bologna and then Parma to complete his artistic education. Thereafter, from his base in Venice, he spent much of his career travelling, working in Rome, Milan, Florence, Vienna and London. He absorbed an unusually broad range of stylistic influences, which are reflected in his own work.

This painting illustrates Christ's miraculous restoration of sight to a blind man at the Pool of Siloam, with the Apostles and a group of sceptical Pharisees looking on (John: 9). With its carefully balanced arrangement, monumental architecture and anecdotal accessory details, Ricci's grand conception of the scene belies its modest scale. It owes a strong debt to similar compositions by the great sixteenth-century artist Paolo Veronese. The painting is first recorded in the collection of the distinguished physician and collector Dr Richard Mead, and in view of its subject-matter it is tempting to suggest that it may have been painted specially for him (as a gift from a grateful patient, perhaps). It probably dates from the time of Ricci's five-year residence in England (1712–16).

Giovanni Battista Pittoni 1687–1767 · The Apotheosis of Saint Jerome with Saint Peter of Alcántara and an Unidentified Franciscan

This altarpiece was painted around 1725 for an altar in the nave of Santa Maria dei Miracoli, one of the most popular and sumptuously decorated small churches in Venice, which was run by Franciscan nuns. The main protagonist of the picture is St Jerome who, with an expression of rapture, is borne aloft on a cloud towards heaven, guided by a guardian angel. Jerome rests his hand on a skull and a rosary, while below appear three of his attributes – a cardinal's hat, a lion, and a large book which alludes to his translation of the Bible. The foreground figure in a brown Franciscan habit and supporting a large cross is the ascetic sixteenth-century Spanish mystic and visionary St Peter of Alcántara, who appears only rarely in Italian art. As if to emphasise the miraculous and spiritual nature of St Jerome's apotheosis, St Peter is shown looking downwards, experiencing the event inwardly without looking at it. A second Franciscan saint or monk gazes on in adoration. The altarpiece is painted in the robust style of Pittoni's early maturity, its strong colours and tonal contrasts and its figure types reflecting the influence of Sebastiano Ricci and the young Tiepolo.

Pittoni was one of the leading exponents of Rococo painting in Venice. Unlike many of his contemporaries, he travelled little, basing himself firmly in his native city. He nevertheless received numerous commissions from elsewhere in Italy and beyond. In their palette, handling and general mood, his mature works often show a close affinity with contemporary French painting.

Oil on canvas (the top originally arched),
275 × 143
Purchased 1960
NG 2238

Giovanni Battista (Giambattista) Tiepolo 1696–1770

The Finding of Moses

Oil on canvas, 202 × 342
Presented to the Royal
Institution by Robert
Clouston 1845; transferred
to the National Gallery
1859
NG 92

Tiepolo was the outstanding Venetian painter and draughtsman of the eighteenth century, and was also a talented printmaker. He was a pupil of Gregorio Lazzarini in his native Venice, but the principal formative influences on his style were the more progressive Sebastiano Ricci, Giambattista Piazzetta and Frederico Bencovich. He was in many respects the artistic heir of the great sixteenth-century master Paolo Veronese. In addition to numerous prestigious secular and religious commissions in Venice, he painted fresco cycles at Udine, in several villas in the Veneto, in Milan and Bergamo, and most famously in the Residenz at Würzburg. Tiepolo was elected president of the Venetian Painters' Academy in 1755. He spent the last eight years of his life working in Madrid at the invitation of King Charles III.

The Finding of Moses is first recorded in the collection of the Venetian patrician Andrea Corner (1672–1742) at Palazzo Corner della Regina on the Grand Canal, and was probably painted for him in the mid-1730s. A section, showing a halberdier and a dog in a river landscape, was removed from the right edge, probably in the early nineteenth century, and is now in a private collection. Although the story of Pharaoh's daughter rescuing the infant Moses from the bulrushes is drawn from the Old Testament, Tiepolo's light-hearted, theatrical treatment of the subject is difficult to take seriously. Moses is shown in a disarmingly realistic and unflattering fashion, upside-down and bawling in distress. Pharaoh's daughter wears a sumptuous golden dress in the sixteenth-century style, whereas the old hag in black, the grotesquely ugly dwarf and the young dandy in pink and blue, could have been borrowed directly from contemporary popular theatre. The overall conception of Tiepolo's Finding of Moses is heavily indebted to Paolo Veronese, although in paying homage he also parodies the sixteenth-century master's treatments of this theme.

In addition to making preparatory drawings, Tiepolo habitually planned his compositions by means of coloured oil sketches on canvas, of which The Meeting of Antony and Cleopatra is a fine example. It shows the encounter between the Roman commander and the Queen of Egypt which is supposed to have taken place in Cilicia in Asia Minor in 41 BC. The sketch relates closely to one of the frescoed scenes carried out around 1745–7 in the grand ballroom of the Palazzo Labia in Venice, the most celebrated secular decorative cycle painted by Tiepolo in his native city. With its rapid, calligraphic brushwork, this sketch is a supreme illustration of Tiepolo's seemingly effortless ability to manipulate form, colour and light into a compelling and harmonious narrative.

The Meeting of Antony and Cleopatra
Oil on canvas, 66.8 × 38.4
Purchased by the Royal Institution, 1845;
transferred to the National Gallery 1857
NG 91

Francesco Guardi 1712–1793
The Piazza San Marco, Venice

Oil on canvas, 55.2 × 85.4
Accepted in lieu of tax 1978
NG 2370

Guardi is the most famous Venetian view painter of the eighteenth century after Canaletto, by whom he was influenced. His father Domenico was a painter of modest talents. Francesco turned to landscape painting around 1750, and is first documented as a painter of *vedute* (topographical views) only in 1764. He had been active during the 1730s and 1740s as a figure painter, often in collaboration with his talented elder brother Gian Antonio. Compared to the crystalline clarity of Canaletto's mature works, Guardi's views of Venice are characterised by a more rapid and impressionistic touch, and a greater feeling for more transient effects of light and atmosphere.

The Piazza San Marco, the hub of Venetian civic and religious life, was painted repeatedly by Guardi from various angles. The main market for these paintings lay with foreign tourists eager for a momento of this spectacular urban space. The Edinburgh painting, which probably dates from about 1775, shows the principal view of the square looking towards the façade of the Basilica of San Marco, its mosaics shimmering in the sunlight. Behind the *campanile* (bell-tower) is a glimpse of the Doge's Palace, while at the sides the view is framed by the receding arcades of the Procuratie Vecchie and Nuove, the former casting a strong shadow over much of the piazza. The scene is enlivened by traders, uniformed government officials, and fashionably dressed tourists and promenaders, all sketched in with a few deft strokes of the brush.

Pompeo Batoni 1708–1787
Portrait of Alexander, 4th Duke of Gordon (1743–1827) 1764

Although rightly best known for his outstanding talents as a portraitist, Batoni's early success was as a history painter. The demand for portraits from his hand rocketed around 1750 and thereafter it became virtually *de rigueur* for distinguished visitors to Rome, especially British and Irish aristocrats on the Grand Tour, to sit to Batoni.

The 4th Duke of Gordon succeeded to the title in 1752 while still a boy. On leaving Eton he received a captain's commission in the 89th Regiment of Foot (the Gordon Highlanders) and was made colonel in 1763. He went on an extended Grand Tour and was in Rome in 1763–4, when this portrait was painted. He served for much of his life as a representative peer for Scotland and held numerous public offices, including Keeper of the Great Seal of Scotland and Lord Lieutenant of Aberdeenshire. In his youth he was reputedly the most handsome man in Scotland.

In Batoni's portrait, the attributes of learning and references to classical antiquity that flatter most of his sitters are absent, and the sitter's passion for field sports and rural pursuits is emphasised instead. Gordon is shown standing elegantly beside his mount, the epitome of aristocratic poise and confidence, with his prized hounds and the spoils of the day's hunt at his feet, and an evocation of Gordon Castle in the distance. The duke was evidently far from overwhelmed by the grandeur of the Eternal City, for according to one report he remained firmly seated in his carriage while the German historian and theorist Winckelmann conducted a tour of its ancient sites. Batoni nevertheless based Gordon's pose loosely on that of a celebrated antique statue, the *Apollo Belvedere*.

Oil on canvas, 292 × 192
Purchased by Private Treaty with the aid of the National Heritage Memorial Fund and the National Art Collections Fund 1994
NG 2589

Antonio Canova 1757–1822 · The Three Graces

Marble, 173 × 97.2 × 75
(maximum dimensions
including base)
Purchased jointly with the
Victoria and Albert
Museum, London, with the
aid of the National Heritage
Memorial Fund, the
National Art Collections
Fund, J. Paul Getty II,
Baron Hans Heinrich
Thyssen-Bornemisza and
public donations 1994
NG 2626

This celebrated masterpiece of neoclassical sculpture was commissioned in January 1815 by John Russell, 6th Duke of Bedford, and his wife Georgiana, who were among the first wave of British visitors to Rome after the hiatus of the Napoleonic wars. Canova was by then the most famous artist in Europe, and distinguished tourists flocked to his studio to meet the great man and order a work from his hand. The Bedfords first made an unsuccessful bid to 'steal' the commission for the first version of The Three Graces group (now in the Hermitage Museum, St Petersburg), which had been ordered by the Empress Josephine in 1813 and which Canova was then completing, after her death, for her son Eugène de Beauharnais. Its final appearance could be gauged from

the full-scale plaster model which Canova made as a standard part of his working procedure, and which survives in the Gipsoteca Canoviana at Possagno, the sculptor's home town on the Venetian mainland. Canova took the opportunity to introduce various improvements in the second version, which was finished by the end of 1817. It was installed in the summer of 1819 in the specially-built Temple of the Graces adjoining the Sculpture Gallery at Woburn Abbey, the Bedfords' country residence. Its pedestal could be rotated to allow viewing from all angles.

The group represents Euphrosyne, Aglaia and Thalia, the three daughters of Zeus and Euryoneme according to Greek mythology. The Three Graces were traditionally associated with Aphrodite, the goddess of love, and have been endowed with a variety of allegorical meanings over the centuries, including reciprocal friendship (giving, receiving and returning); chastity, beauty and love; three aspects of beauty; and so forth. Canova's treatment of the Three Graces theme departed from antique and renaissance precedents, which invariably showed them in a more rigid arrangement, completely naked and with the central Grace facing the opposite way to her sisters. He conceived instead a close-knit group, arranged in a loose semi-circle and bonded together by complementary poses and gazes, interlacing arms and a beautifully carved rope of drapery. Behind them to one side is a cylindrical altar draped with a garland of flowers. When viewed under the intended conditions – softly illuminated from above in diffuse natural light – the sophistication of Canova's evocation of palpable flesh from cold marble is breathtaking.

Note: The Three Graces are on display alternately at the National Gallery of Scotland and the Victoria and Albert Museum, London, for periods of seven years.

El Greco 1541–1614

An Allegory ('Fábula')
Oil on canvas, 67.3 × 88.6
Accepted in lieu of tax, with
additional funding from the
National Heritage
Memorial Fund, the
National Art Collections
Fund and Gallery funds
1989
NG 2491

His real name was Domenikos Theotokopoulos, but he is universally known by his Spanish sobriquet, El Greco ('the Greek'). He was trained in the Byzantine tradition of his native Crete, but his style transformed after he moved to Venice (by 1568), where he was reportedly a pupil of Titian. He was in Rome in the service of the Farnese family by 1570, and in 1577 he settled permanently in Toledo in Spain. Within a few years he had perfected his highly idiosyncratic mature style which remained essentially unchanged until his death. The output of his Toledo workshop was prodigious, with many compositions surviving in multiple versions.

The mysterious Fábula, the meaning of which has remained elusive, is the latest of three versions of this composition, the earliest of which (Museo del Prado, Madrid) probably dates from El Greco's Roman period. This in turn was partly based on a painting of A Boy Lighting a Candle (Museo Nazionale di Capodimonte, Naples), which was inspired by Pliny the Elder's written description of a lost painting from antiquity. In the context of the Edinburgh Allegory, the act of kindling flames may allude to the arousal of sensual passions. A monkey in art is often symbolic of vice, while the man in the yellow cloak grinning inanely may represent folly. The painting may thus convey the simple moralising message that lust appeals to our foolish and baser instincts, although the possibility that it is an illustration of a proverb or fable cannot be ruled out. Whatever its significance, it was no doubt destined for the collection of a learned individual with

Christ Blessing ('The Saviour of the World')
Oil on canvas, 73 × 56.5
Purchased 1952
NG 2160

sophisticated tastes: one version of the composition belonged during El Greco's lifetime to San Juan de Ribera, Patriarch of Antioch and Archbishop of Valencia.

The pale, gaunt *Saviour of the World* is shown with his right hand raised in the Latin gesture of benediction, while the spidery fingers of his left hand rest on the crystalline orb of the world. The direct, frontal presentation of Christ recalls the hieratic Byzantine tradition of El Greco's youth, although in the Eastern Church he would normally have been shown as 'Pantocrator', with a book rather than a globe. The painting may originally have formed part of a series of Christ with the twelve Apostles, known in Spain as *Apostolados*. Two three-quarter-length series of this kind by El Greco survive.

Diego Velázquez 1599–1660
An Old Woman Cooking Eggs 1618

Oil on canvas,
100.5 × 119.5 cm
Purchased with the aid of
the National Art Collections
Fund and a Treasury Grant
1955
NG 2180

Dated 1618, this remarkable picture was painted when Velázquez was just eighteen or nineteen, shortly after he had completed his apprenticeship with the painter and writer Francisco Pacheco, whose daughter he married in the same year. It is one of a small group of kitchen and tavern scenes (*bodegones* in Spanish) painted by Velázquez in his native Seville before he moved permanently to the court of Philip IV in Madrid in 1623. Although Velázquez's *bodegones* were influenced in some respects by Flemish and Italian genre paintings, the mood he created was quite new and the skill with which he painted them was completely unprecedented in Spain.

The old woman and the boy in this painting were real people and they both reappear in other early works by Velázquez. They were evidently posed in his studio and painted directly from life, much as the still-life elements would have been. Velázquez was clearly fascinated by the contrasting materials and textures of these simple vessels, implements and foods, and especially by their varied responses to bright illumination. Particularly impressive are the semi-solidified egg-whites in the glazed terracotta dish, and the differing degrees to which the burnished brass bowl and the matt pestle and mortar reflect the light. The virtuoso rendition of these objects seems almost to have been an end in itself. Domestic scenes comparable to this appear in Spanish picaresque novels of this period, notably in Mateo Alemán's popular *Guzmán de Alfarache* (1599), but it is unlikely that *An Old Woman Cooking Eggs* illustrates a specific text.

The Edinbugh painting is probably identical with one of this subject listed in two inventories dating from the 1690s of the possessions of the Sevillian merchant, collector and patron of Murillo, Nicolás Omazur.

Francisco de Zurbarán 1598–1664
The Immaculate Conception with Saints Joachim and Anne

Zurbarán was born in the province of Extremadura, but he trained in Seville and was to base himself there for most of his career. He had a brief spell at the court of Philip IV in Madrid in 1634–5, and returned there at the end of his life after his once dominant position in Seville had been eclipsed by Murillo and other younger painters. Zurbarán is best known as a 'painter of monks' on account of the many monastic commissions he received, but he also painted numerous more public religious works and a few exquisite still lifes. During the 1640s his workshop specialised in the production of series paintings for export to the New World.

The subject of the Immaculate Conception – which refers not to the conception of Christ, but to the Virgin's own miraculous conception in the womb of her mother Anne – became especially popular in Seville following the publication there in 1617 of a papal bull prohibiting denial of this mystery. It was painted several times by Zurbarán, but the Edinburgh version is unique in its inclusion of the Virgin's parents, Joachim and Anne, in a manner reminiscent of donor portraits. The statuesque Virgin is shown perched on a pedestal of cherubs' heads above a crescent moon, bathed in golden light. Saints Joachim and Anne were particularly venerated by the Carthusian order, and their presence in this painting has led to the suggestion that it may have been one of a series executed by Zurbarán in the late 1630s for the Carthusian monastery at Jerez de la Frontera, near Cadiz. However, the scant documentary evidence available rather undermines this hypothesis.

Oil on canvas, 255.5 × 177
Purchased by the Royal Institution, 1859;
transferred to the National Gallery 1867
NG 340

Bartolomé Esteban Murillo 1617–1682
A Young Man with a Basket of Fruit (Personification of Summer)

Oil on canvas, 102 × 81.5
Purchased by Private Treaty
with the aid of the National
Art Collections Fund 1999
NG 2706

This recently rediscovered picture is an important addition to Murillo's secular oeuvre and is one of very few paintings by him with overtly allegorical subject-matter. The youth is identified as a *Personification of Summer* by virtue of the basket of seasonal fruit and vegetables, and especially the ears of barley protruding from his turban (*Autumn* would traditionally have been associated with the grape harvest). The rarity of such subjects by Murillo makes it highly likely that the Edinburgh painting is identical with one representing *Summer* listed, together with a figure of *Spring*, in the posthumous inventory (1685) of Justino de Neve, whose full-length portrait by Murillo is in the National Gallery, London. Both pictures evidently passed into the collection of another of the artist's most important patrons, Nicolás Omazur, where they joined paintings of *Autumn* and *Winter* to complete a set of the four seasons.

A generation younger than his compatriot Velázquez, Murillo's entire career was centred on his native Seville. He was influenced early on by Zurbarán, whom he came first to rival and later surpass as the leading painter in the city. Murillo's fame rests largely on his enormous output of altarpieces, devotional works and cycles of religious narratives, but he also painted some fine portraits and genre scenes. Many of Murillo's secular pictures were purchased by foreign merchants resident in the city, and in the eighteenth and nineteenth century they were especially popular with British collectors and artists.

Francisco de Goya 1746–1828
El Médico (The Doctor)

Equally accomplished as a painter and printmaker, Goya was one of the most original and enigmatic artists of his age. He was from the province of Zaragoza in north-eastern Spain, but settled in Madrid in 1774 and worked there for most of his career. He supplied numerous designs for the Royal Tapestry Works, and was appointed painter to the king in 1786. A serious illness in 1793 left him permanently deaf. He remained in Madrid during the French occupation (1808–13) and again worked for the Spanish monarchy after its restoration. He spent the last years of his life in Bordeaux in France.

El Médico is a tapestry cartoon that Goya delivered, together with ten others, to the Royal Tapestry Factory in January 1780. The related tapestry formed part of the decoration of the Ante-Dormitorio of the Prince and Princess of Asturias in the royal palace of El Pardo. Goya had already furnished tapestry designs for two other rooms in these apartments, and the three series illustrated the broad theme of the diversions, customs and fashions of the time.

The final tapestry of El Médico was to be hung above a door, and Goya took account of this high location: the viewpoint is low, the design relatively simple, the colours bold, and the few bulky figures silhouetted clearly against the sky. Goya's invoice for the painting describes the subject as 'A doctor seated, warming himself at a brazier; some books on the ground by his side, behind him two students', the relevance of which to the theme of the room is unclear, although it has been noted that a man warming his hands and a leafless tree are both emblems of winter.

Oil on canvas,
95.8 × 120.2 (cut down from about 100 × 150)
Purchased 1923
NG 1628

Hugo van der Goes active 1467–died 1482 · The Trinity Altarpiece

Left wing
The Holy Trinity of the Broken Body
Right wing
Edward Bonkil with Two Angels
Left wing reverse
James III, King of Scots (1452–88) with his son James (?) presented by St Andrew
Right wing reverse
Margaret of Denmark, Queen of Scots (1456–86), presented by St George (?)
Oil on panel, 202 × 100.5 (each panel)
Lent by Her Majesty The Queen

This is the most important surviving altarpiece ever to have been commissioned for Scotland. It was painted by Hugo van der Goes, one of the greatest masters of early Netherlandish art who was a lay-brother in the Rode Klooster monastery near Brussels. Hugo's painting combined the exquisitely depicted naturalistic detail of the brothers Hubert and Jan van Eyck, and the deep pathos of Rogier van der Weyden. In the late fifteenth century, the Netherlands were a lively centre of trade and Hugo's works were bought by aristocrats and merchants throughout Europe. The altarpiece he painted for a member of the Portinari family of 1473–8 (Uffizi, Florence), is closely

related to *The Trinity Altarpiece* in date and style, and was described by the artist Giorgio Vasari in 1550. It remains the only work which can certainly be attributed to Hugo, but *The Trinity Altarpiece* is also universally accepted as an authentic work.

When the wings are closed, the oak panel on the left shows the Holy Trinity as a heavenly vision, seen by Provost Edward Bonkil on the right, commissioner of the panels for the Collegiate Chapel of the Holy Trinity (once in the centre of Edinburgh but almost completely demolished in 1848). He also paid for an organ for the chapel – hence the presence of the splendid gilded instrument by him in

the painting. The chapel was founded by the mother of King James III. His portrait and that of his queen appear on the inside of the panels. On the left with St Andrew, patron saint of Scotland, is the king's first son, born in 1473. The panels were probably painted four or five years later, given the prince's apparent age, but presumably before the birth of his brother in 1478 (who was likely to have been included here as part of the dynasty had he been born when it was painted).

The royal faces are very 'wooden', clearly copied from another source, contrasting with the life-like portrait of Bonkil. He may have travelled to the Low Countries to sit for his likeness, especially as a probable relative of his was the king's unofficial envoy in Flanders at the time. It is rare for religious images to have survived the Reformation and the presence of royal portraits is probably the only reason these panels remained in existence. There was almost certainly once a central panel, perhaps a *Virgin and Child Enthroned*, which failed to escape iconoclastic attack. This is implied by the monarchs praying towards the centre and even the lion on the king's coat of arms, which usually faces the other way, here looks to his left in order not to turn his back on the now missing central holy figures.

Gerard David c.1460–1523 · Three Legends of St Nicholas

Left

He gives thanks to God on the day of his birth

Centre

He slips a purse through the window of an impoverished nobleman as dowry for his daughters

Right

As Bishop of Myra, he resuscitates three boys salted down as meat in a famine

Oil on panel, 55.9 × 33.7 (each panel)

Purchased with the aid of the National Art Collections Fund and a Treasury Grant 1959

NG 2213

These panels originally formed part of a very large altarpiece depicting the *Virgin and Child with Saint Anne, St Nicholas of Myra and St Anthony of Padua* that was painted by David with help from artists in his workshop sometime between 1500 and 1520. (The other panels are in the National Gallery of Art, Washington, and Toledo Museum, Ohio.) St Nicholas, was Archbishop of Myra in Asia Minor in the fourth century. He appears in the left panel as a miraculously precocious baby praying in his bath. Better known to us as Santa Claus, the kindly patron of children, he is next shown saving three girls from prostitution by giving money for their dowries. In the third panel, shown in bishop's robes, he revives three murdered boys.

David was born in Gouda but moved to Bruges where he joined the artists' guild in 1484. He was inspired by the earlier great masters Van Eyck and Van der Goes but developed his own unique style and, after the death of Hans Memling in 1494, he became the key painter in Bruges. His work-shop employed a number of assistants from about 1498–9 to help him fulfil the considerable demand for his work.

These little panels are the same format as three more at Toledo depicting scenes from the life of St Anthony of Padua. All six were probably fixed to the bottom of the large Washington panels forming what is called a *predella*. This style of large non-folding altarpiece was common in southern Europe but rarer in the north, which suggests that it may have been commissioned for someone in Spain or Italy. The commission may have had a specific connection with children as both St Nicholas and St Anthony are famous for their kindness to the young.

Quentin Massys (also Quinten Metsys) 1466–1530 · *Portrait of a Man*

Oil on panel, 80 × 64.5
Accepted in lieu of tax 1965
NG 2273

Painted between 1510 and 1520, this was once thought to portray St Fiacre (patron of notaries) or, possibly, a member of the Rosicrucian religious sect (hence the rose and the cross). However, X-rays revealed that all the objects in front of the sitter and the halo, quill and cross were added to the original portrait probably sometime after completion. The young man was originally holding only a rosebud, a common symbol of love (though also sometimes of the transience of beauty, and life).

What is certain is the high quality of the painting and the wealth of the sitter. Massys was much admired in Antwerp as a painter of religious subjects but also as a portraitist of distinction – his painting of Erasmus, executed in 1517, and given to that other great humanist, Sir Thomas More, is a good example of this skill. This type of 'head-and-shoulders' portrait set against a landscape background was developed from innovative examples by Memling and Van Eyck. The Netherlandish tradition of portraiture was much emulated by artists all over Europe, though Massys, in turn, was aware of Italian painting (especially that of Leonardo) which informed his work.

Joos van Cleve active 1505/08–died 1540/1 · *Triptych*

Centre
The Deposition from the Cross
Left wing
St John the Baptist with a Donor
Right wing
St Margaret of Antioch with a Donatrix
Oil on panel, 106.7 × 71.1 centre; 109.2 × 31.8 wings
Purchased 1920
NG 1252

One of the most important artists working in Antwerp at the beginning of the sixteenth century, Joos's work demonstrates knowledge of Van der Goes and Van Eyck. But, like his contemporary Quentin Massys, he also showed an awareness of Italian art, particularly that of Leonardo da Vinci, especially apparent in his much-copied Madonnas. Here, however, he shows artistic kinship with the group known as the Antwerp Mannerists, with whom he shared a delight in the depiction of complicated costume and multi-faceted surface detail, such as elaborate folds of material, or the richly gilded headdress of St Margaret. She is here shown with the satanic dragon from whose belly she was miraculously freed. Many expectant mothers prayed to her that their baby would, similarly, be safely delivered – a not unreason-

able concern in an age in which childbirth was frequently fatal. The composition of this altarpiece relates closely in style to the slightly earlier *Crucifixion* triptych now in the Museo di Capodimonte, Naples (1518/19) and was probably commissioned shortly after this by Antwerp donors.

Joos's real surname was Van der Beke but he was nicknamed Cleve after the area in north Rhine-Westphalia from which he presumably came before becoming a guild member in Antwerp in 1511. He was also a gifted portraitist and worked at the French court (and perhaps in Italy) possibly between 1529 and 1534.

Bernard van Orley c.1488–1541 · *Before the Crucifixion*

Van Orley came from Brussels and became court painter to Margaret of Austria, Regent of the Spanish Netherlands, in 1518. His work was much influenced by Italian Renaissance art, notably by Raphael. He ran a flourishing workshop, also designing tapestry and stained glass with which he became more involved from about 1520. While the Netherlands were ruled by the Catholic Spanish Habsburgs, many rich Spanish aristocrats and merchants travelled to the region, then famous as a centre of international trade. Many splendid examples of early Netherlandish art can still be found in Spain today as a result.

This panel was originally one of a set of four scenes painted for Henry III, Count of Nassau, and his third wife Mencia de Mendoza, whom he married in Spain in 1522. The bound, seated, pose of Christ was very unusual in a painting of this type. The other panels showed an *Agony in the Garden*, the *Crowning with Thorns*, and *Christ Carrying the Cross*. All bear traces of the same coat of arms and must date from between 1530, when Henry arrived back in the Netherlands, and 1535, when the finished works had been delivered to Mencia's castle in Jadraque in Spain. Mencia remained an important patron for Van Orley: in 1539 she commissioned him to produce a series of small tapestry cartoons for her family's funerary chapel in Valencia.

Oil on panel, 67.3 × 85.7
Purchased 1909
NG 995

Denys Calvaert 1540–1619
The Holy Family with the Infant St John the Baptist in a Landscape

Oil on copper, 42 × 32
Purchased with the aid of
the Patrons of the National
Galleries of Scotland and the
National Art Collections
Fund 1987
NG 2447

Calvaert was born in Antwerp but spent most of his professional life as a painter and draughtsman in Italy. He founded an academy in Bologna and was one of the most successful artists there towards the end of the sixteenth century. His work was almost entirely religious and ranged from large altarpieces to small highly finished paintings like this one. These were often painted on copper, a support that Calvaert may have introduced to Bologna; he certainly popularised its use there. This had a significant influence upon a generation of Bolognese artists, most notably Guido Reni, Francesco Albani and Domenichino, all of whom painted the 'little copper of the Flemish' as the contemporary critic Malvasia called such pieces. Copper with its smooth hard surface was the perfect support for the deft fluidity and clear contours of Calvaert's designs, giving a bright jewel-like finish to his glowing colours.

The scene depicted here is not mentioned in the Bible. Calvaert sets it in typically verdant landscape in the Flemish style with angels providing fruit and spring water, while above appears a miraculous vision of the Cross. Calvaert often re-used the same composition in his works and there are two other close variants of the Edinburgh painting, both dating to c.1590–1600, and at least three related sketches. The numbers produced imply that they were extremely popular as private devotional images.

Jacques de Gheyn the Younger 1565–1629
Studies of a Frog

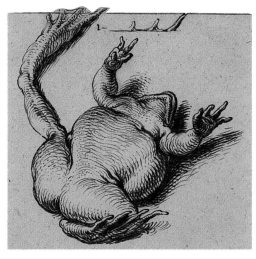

Pen and brown ink on paper,
15.7 × 12.1 (left), 12.1 × 13.1 (right)
Purchased 1979
D 5077A, B

These sketches of a frog – its slack skin rendered by lively hooked strokes of the pen imitating engraved lines – were made 'after the life' or in this case, perhaps, after the death of the hapless specimen. They do not seem to have been made as studies for a print or painting. Another sheet, in Amsterdam's Rijksprentenkabinet, with four watercolour studies of a similar frog is annotated with the creature's measurements. Such details, together with the obvious desire for verisimilitude, mark these studies as virtually scientific records, which had their precursors in detailed drawings after nature made by earlier northern artists such as Albrecht Dürer. The Edinburgh sketches were probably made c.1595–8 when De Gheyn lived in Leiden, then a centre for the study of natural history. He was sufficiently acquainted with the circle of scientists there to make a portrait of the celebrated botanist Carolus Clusius.

The Amsterdam watercolour, however, probaly dates from a little later as it is almost certainly related to a whole album of studies of flora and fauna De Gheyn made between 1600 and 1604, reputedly bought by the great collector Emperor Rudolf II.

In about 1585, De Gheyn had left Antwerp to join the Haarlem studio of the great artist and draughtsman Hendrik Goltzius (1558–1617). Haarlem was then the most important artistic centre in the northern Netherlands, largely due to Goltzius whose Mannerist compositions with exaggerated figures were widely known through prints. De Gheyn was particularly influenced by Goltzius in his printmaking, which gained De Gheyn great renown (though he later concentrated on painting from c.1600). From 1598, he worked in The Hague for Maurits, Prince of Orange, and later for his successor, Prince Frederik Hendrik.

Paul Bril 1553/4–1626 · *Fantastic Landscape* 1598

Oil on copper, 21.3 × 29.2
Bequest of Mrs Nisbet
Hamilton Ogilvy of Biel
1921
NG 1492

Bril was one of the many artists attracted to Rome, by its magnificent art and architecture and the tempting possibility of papal and aristocratic commissions. He set off from Antwerp to join his elder brother, Matthijs (c.1550–1583), arriving in Rome by 1582 where he spent the rest of his life. Bril was a key figure for generations of northern artists who visited Rome and his influential landscape style was relayed back to the Netherlands by them and via prints. He, in turn, was sometimes affected by the work of other painters such as Adam Elsheimer, who was a close friend. He also knew Rubens during his stay in the city.

This imaginary scene is a characteristic example of Bril's landscape style of the 1590s. The high viewpoint, fantastical rocky outcrops, steep-sided valley, and the bands of different colours which suggest recession into the distance are all features of the Antwerp landscape tradition in which he had been trained. He incorporated details of classical architecture, sketched in Rome, a practice copied from Mattijs. This innovative combination influenced the development of landscape painting both in Italy and further north. In addition to small pictures on copper like this one, Bril painted a number of frescoes, mainly in the Vatican, executed in a broader style. Some of his works are signed with the visual pun of a pair of spectacles, the Dutch word for which is 'Bril'.

Hendrick Avercamp 1585–1634 · *Winter Landscape*

Avercamp was the first artist in the northern Netherlands to paint winter scenes, little pictures like this which would not have been commissioned but offered for general sale. Avercamp was probably influenced by the snowy landscapes of the sixteenth-century Flemish master Pieter Bruegel the Elder. He may have met Bruegel's Flemish followers, Gillis Coninxloo, Hans Bol, and David Vinckboons, in Amsterdam, where they fled after the Spanish invasion of Antwerp in 1585. The mainly Protestant northern Netherlands (later called the United Provinces or the Dutch Republic), won secession from Catholic Spanish rule in 1609. From about this period the art of the northern (Dutch) and southern (Spanish-Flemish) Netherlands became increasingly different. The latter retained the patronage of both the Catholic Church and the Spanish court, while the Calvinist Dutch Republic encouraged the development of a different art, celebrating national identity through landscape paintings and seascapes, architectural views and specific historical, biblical and moralising scenes.

Apart from training in Amsterdam, the deaf-mute Avercamp spent most of his life in the tranquil walled town of Kampen, on the Zuider Zee. Kampen can be seen in the background of this mature work of the early 1620s. Despite the vivid nature of the scene, this would have been painted in the studio though Avercamp did make studies from nature, sometimes incorporating elements from these into his paintings. The white crescent sign on the inn at the left may allude to Kampen's Half Moon brewery.

Oil on copper, 28.6 × 42.2
Bequest of David Laing
1879
NG 647

Sir Peter Paul Rubens 1577–1640 · A Study of a Head (St Ambrose)

Oil on panel, 49.6 × 38.1
Purchased with the aid of the Cowan Smith
Bequest Fund 1947
NG 2097

The most learned, inventive and productive artist in the history of the northern Baroque, Rubens's talent was extraordinary. The range of his work was colossal, encompassing portraiture, allegory, religious painting, landscapes, and designs for ornament, tapestry, books and prints. A diplomat and scholar, his intelligent use of iconography was never rivalled, perfectly matching allusions to a patron's aspirations, while his emotive religious works were actively intended as part of the Catholic armoury against the onslaught of the Protestant Reformation. Having trained in Antwerp, Rubens spent from 1600 to 1608 in Italy (made a brief visit to Spain), returned to Flanders in 1608 and was appointed non-resident court painter to the Catholic Archdukes Albert and Isabella in 1609. His Antwerp studio was run on an almost industrial scale, with numerous assistants, including Anthony van Dyck and Jacob Jordaens.

This is a preparatory study for the head of St Ambrose in the large altarpiece of *St Ambrose Refusing the Emperor Theodosius Admission to the Church of Milan* (Kunsthistorisches Museum, Vienna) of about 1618. Ambrose, fourth-century Archbishop of Milan, stood firm against Theodosius in outrage against the emperor's Thessalonican massacre. The vividness of the brushstrokes and animation of the face in the Edinburgh picture imply that it was studied from a living model. The finished work in Vienna was once thought to be by Van Dyck (who painted a reworked version now in the National Gallery, London) but it is now generally agreed that Rubens was actually heavily involved in the project. There is certainly no doubt about his authorship of the Edinburgh study.

Sir Peter Paul Rubens 1577–1640 · The Reconciliation of Jacob and Esau

Oil on panel, 42.5 × 40.3
Accepted in lieu of tax 1980
NG 2397

Oil studies played an important part in the efficient functioning of Rubens's phenomenally busy studio, where delegation was essential to complete the numerous prestigious commissions he was so successful in securing from the Catholic Church and the sovereigns of France, Spain and England. He made many studies of this kind to work out the design of a large painting or decorative scheme. These studies were then often shown to the patron for approval but were also a guide to assistants when working up paintings from Rubens's designs. This study would have represented the design for the final picture for which it was the model (hence the term 'modello' sometimes used for these studies). Connoisseurs have always prized studies like this where the vibrant and fluent brushstrokes ensure that the work is from Rubens's hand alone.

Painted in about 1624, it shows Jacob making peace with his twin brother, many years after stealing Esau's birthright by deception (Genesis: 33). It is a study for a picture now in the Alte Pinakothek, Munich, and there are few differences between the study and the finished painting. The Munich picture, which included some workshop participation, was one of eight large canvases Rubens took with him on his diplomatic mission to the court of Philip IV in Spain in 1628.

Sir Peter Paul Rubens 1577–1640 · *The Feast of Herod*

Oil on canvas, 208 × 264
Purchased 1958
NG 2193

Herodias, through her daughter Salome, forced her husband Herod Antipas to order the death of John the Baptist. The story is described in the New Testament (Mark 6:14–29 and Matthew 14:1–12) though Salome is not mentioned by name. In this picture Herodias spears St John's tongue with a fork, in revenge for his speaking out against her, a gesture first described by St Jerome who compared it to Fulvia mocking the severed head of Cicero in Dio Cassius's *History of Rome*. The composition was engraved in extended format and much copied. Probably painted 1635–8, the picture was in Naples by 1640 where it demonstrably influenced a generation of Neapolitan painters such as Mattia Preti and Luca Giordano. It was in a collection which included works by these artists, owned by the Flemish merchant Gaspar de Roomer, who exported Neapolitan art to the Low Countries. He could well have commissioned this picture when visiting Antwerp and the somewhat gory nature of the subject would have fitted well with his other paintings which revealed a penchant for 'the grotesque, dark and cruel'.

The level of studio involvement in the Edinburgh *Feast of Herod* has been the subject of much debate. Rubens's enormous commissions, for the Cardinal Infante Ferdinand during 1634–5 and for Philip IV from 1636, involved considerable workshop assistance. After his second marriage in 1630, Rubens spent more time with his family and considerably less time working officially in the studio, particularly after 1635, when he bought Château de Steen, the country estate that inspired his finest landscapes.

Sir Anthony van Dyck 1599–1641 · Saint Sebastian Bound for Martyrdom

It is for his elegant portraits of the court of Charles I, glamorous yet poignant images which define an age, that Van Dyck is most famous. But despite revolutionising portraiture in Britain, Van Dyck trained in Antwerp and, as befitted that tradition, he also painted many impressive religious, allegorical and mythological works and landscapes. He had studied with Hendrik van Balen, becoming Rubens's chief assistant from 1617 to 1620. After a brief visit to England, Van Dyck then spent a period in Italy (1621–7), returning to Antwerp for five years before moving to England in 1632.

St Sebastian, condemned for his Christianity, was usually shown with arrows piercing his body, but (following Wenzel Cobergher's unusual *Saint Sebastian* once in Antwerp Cathedral) Van Dyck has shown him being prepared for martyrdom. The young artist frequently created variant versions of a composition and he painted several versions of this subject between 1615 and 1621. Technical examination shows that this composition was originally based on an earlier work (c.1615–6) now in the Louvre (for which there is a study in Dublin). There is some debate over the precise sequence of the versions but it seems that his St Sebastian in the Alte Pinakotek, Munich, and the study for it in the Chrysler Museum (Norfolk, USA), may predate the Edinburgh version. Van Dyck probably reworked this canvas (1620–21) and the fact that he kept revisiting, changing, repainting the subject suggests that it was one he found strangely compelling.

Oil on canvas, 226 × 160
Purchased by the Royal Institution 1830;
transferred to the National Gallery 1859
NG 121

Sir Anthony van Dyck 1599–1641 · 'The Lomellini Family'

Oil on canvas, 269 × 254
Purchased by the Royal
Institution 1830;
transferred to the National
Gallery 1859
NG 120

The young Van Dyck, 'best assistant' of Rubens in Antwerp, followed the latter's example by making a prolonged stay in Italy to perfect his art. He travelled extensively but used Genoa, then one of the richest ports in Europe, as his base from 1621 to 1627. It was his experience of portraying the city's sophisticated élite that was to make Van Dyck the obvious choice of court painter for Charles I in London from 1632.

This is Van Dyck's grandest, most ambitious portrait of aristocratic Genoese patrons. The picture was in the Palazzo Lomellini in Genoa in 1827 where it was copied by the Scottish artist Sir David Wilkie. It was purchased from there in 1830. Research in Genoa indicates that the sitters were almost certainly the family of Giacomo Lomellini (1570–1652), Doge of Genoa from 1625 to 1627. Giacomo does not appear in the painting himself – tradition forbade portraits of the doge in office in order to prevent personal propaganda – but Van Dyck nonetheless perfectly captures the family's status and dynastic intent. Those portrayed are probably Nicolò (born 1590) at the left, with his brother Giovanni Francesco (born 1601), with their father's second wife, Barbara Spinola, with the children Vittoria (born c.1620) and Agostino (born 1622) shown at the right of the picture.

Probably painted 1626–7, the painting is effectively a manifesto of the importance of the Lomellini in the city of Genoa. The armour worn by the doge's eldest son may refer to the family's involvement in the defence of the city against an invasion of Protestants from Piedmont. The doge himself had laid the first stone of a new city fortification wall on 7

December 1626. At the same time, family life is celebrated by the presence of Barbara and her young children. A classical statue of the Venus Pudica, chaste protector of the family, appears in the background behind them. The implication is of the Lomellini as defenders, not only of the family and the city of Genoa, but also of the Catholic faith: protectors of both body and soul.

Jacob Jordaens 1593–1678 · Female Nude, Seen from the Back

Black, red and white chalk
on paper, 25.7 × 20.3
David Laing; his bequest to
the Royal Scottish
Academy, 1879; transferred
to the National Gallery
1910
D 1696

Jordaens acted as an independent assistant to Rubens from 1623 to 1633. After the latter's death in 1640, he became the leading artist in Antwerp and the southern Netherlands, although he failed to attract the same volume of courtly patronage as Rubens or Van Dyck. Jordaens was a painter, draughtsman and designer of tapestries who produced religious and historical works but he is perhaps best known for his earthy portrayals of popular proverbs.

Jordaens bought a large house in Antwerp in 1639, which he decorated with twelve paintings of his own which depicted the signs of the zodiac, painted in about 1641. This drawing was a preparatory study for a mythological scene portraying the astrological sign of Capricorn (and the month December), usually represented by a goat. It showed the nymph Adrastea milking the goat Amalthea in order to feed the infant Jupiter. Inspired by Rubens's technique, the skilled use of chalks in this impressive drawing shows the artist at the height of his powers. Jordaens's family sold the house in 1708, but the zodiac pictures were bought in 1802 by the French State to decorate the ceiling of what became the Bibliothèque du Sénat in the Palais du Luxembourg in Paris, where they remain today.

Frans Hals c.1580/85–1666 · *Verdonck*

Frans Hals was the unequalled master of portraiture in Haarlem in the seventeenth century. He is famous for his accomplished and animated likenesses of the city's regent class, militia and wealthy merchants, but he also painted a number of genre scenes and some religious works.

This is an extraordinary work in Hals's oeuvre. Painted in about 1627, the sitter does not personify the predictable propriety of a Haarlem burgher. The composition was engraved by Jan van de Velde II (1593–1641), together with the verse 'This is Verdonck, that outspoken fellow whose jawbone attacks all. He cares for nobody, great or small – that's what brought him to prison.' Verdonck has been identified as the aggressively argumentative Pieter Verdonck, a prominent member of the most puritanical group of Mennonites in Haarlem, who bludgeoned his enemies with his words as effectively as Samson smote the Philistines with his ass's jawbone. Hals presumably could not procure the latter as his model for the gruesome cudgel here is the jawbone of a cow. In 1628 Verdonck was ordered not to molest physically a member of an opposing Mennonite group, the same group which was later violently lambasted in a pamphlet of 1636 entitled *Het Kakebeen* ('The Jawbone') so this attribute would have been considered appropriate. The verse on Van de Velde's engraving implies Verdonck may have been arrested for such transgressions. He still had the capacity to offend in the nineteenth century when repaints were deemed necessary to 'gentrify' him into '*The Toper*', obscuring his hair with a beret, and the jawbone with a wineglass – additions which were removed in 1928.

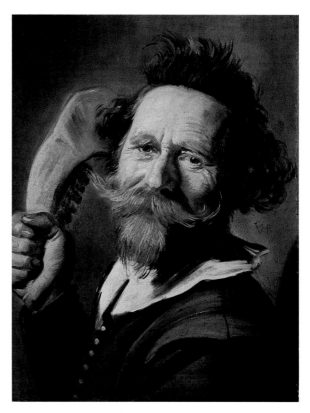

Oil on panel, 46.7 × 35.5
Presented by John J. Moubray of Naemoor 1916
NG 1200

Jan Lievens 1607–1674 · *Portrait of a Young Man*

Oil on canvas, 112 × 99.4
Purchased with the aid of
the Cowan Smith Bequest
Fund 1922
NG 1564

The young Lievens and Rembrandt were once regarded as worthy equals. The Prince of Orange bought works from them both and his secretary, Constantijn Huyghens, wrote a contemporary critique of the two young artists, stating that while Rembrandt might be superior to Lievens in his ability to show 'liveliness of emotions' and 'vivid invention' in history painting, Lievens was 'the greater in inventiveness and audacious themes and forms'.

Lievens was apprenticed in Amsterdam with Pieter Lastman from 1617 to 1619 (where Rembrandt was to train in 1623), returning then to his native city of Leiden as an independent master, as Rembrandt also later did. The two were keenly competitive, their close rivalry spurring them on to greater originality,

each trying to outdo the other. Both artists then shared a common preoccupation with the rendering of light in paint. Lievens manages to make the half-lit face and soft surface of the rich material glow with a hidden light in this dramatic painting, which is arguably his masterpiece, painted c.1631. The subject of the work is not known, though the costume is clearly intentionally exotic, and Lievens may have used himself as a model. After Rembrandt left to settle in Amsterdam towards the end of 1631, the intensity of competitive creativity evaporated for Lievens, and he left for England the following year. Though always competent and successful, Lievens never completely fulfilled the extraordinary promise of his youthful work which shines from this painting.

Gerrit Dou 1613–1675 · An Interior with a Young Violinist, 1637

The first of the Leiden *Fijnschilders* (fine painters), Dou influenced a whole school of artists, his pupils including Frans van Mieris and Godfried Schalcken. His precision of detail and ability to suggest textures with almost photographic accuracy – the shine upon silver and the sheen upon silk, for example – were much admired and emulated, and are elements now often thought of as typical of the Dutch school. Born in Leiden and apprenticed to his father, a glazier, in 1628 Dou went to study with Rembrandt, also a native of Leiden. He remained for three years until Rembrandt's departure for Amsterdam, after which Dou developed the meticulous style for which he became famous.

This is the earliest dated painting by Dou, though earlier undated ones have survived. The picture was probably bought for Queen Christina of Sweden by Pieter Spiering sometime between 1637 and 1645 when he was Swedish ambassador to the Netherlands. Dou later specialised in this type of genre scene, painting fewer portraits and *tronies* (studies of heads) after the 1640s. The still-life elements point to some symbolic significance and there was a strong tradition for such allegorical works in Leiden, though the exact meaning of this picture is unclear. The student surrounded by books, music and the globe might embody some allegory of learning, particularly appropriate in Leiden the university city.

Oil on panel, 31.1 × 23.7 (arched top)
Purchased with the aid of the National Heritage Memorial Fund 1984
NG 2420

Pieter Jansz. Saenredam 1597–1665
The Interior of St Bavo's Church, Haarlem (the 'Grote Kerk') 1648

Oil on panel,
174.8 × 143.6
Purchased by Private Treaty
with the aid of the National
Heritage Memorial Fund,
the National Art Collections
Fund (William Leng
Bequest) and the Pilgrim
Trust 1982
NG 2413

This is the largest and grandest of Saenredam's works on panel. It depicts St Bavo's Cathedral, one of the finest Gothic buildings in the Netherlands, begun in 1397. The artist, who was born in Assendelft, the son of the engraver Jan Saenredam, spent most of his life in Haarlem and was ultimately buried in this church. He trained in the city in Frans Pietersz. de Grebber's studio from 1612 to 1622, becoming a guild member in 1623. Although his earliest dated picture of 1626 was of a religious subject, the architectural pieces in which he was to specialise are some of the most distinctive in Dutch art. A friend of Jacob van Campen, the architect of Amsterdam's town hall, Saenredam was one of the first artists to employ measured drawings in his compositions which were prized for their mastery of perspective.

St Bavo's is virtually unchanged today, apart from the removal of the fifteenth-century organ. Saenredam's signature appears on a column as if in graffiti, together with the date of 27 February 1648 and a scribbled sketch of a man with a bird that may represent St Bavo with his falcon. Saenredam made a preliminary sketch of the church on 25 August 1635, and a more precise perspectival study on 15 December 1635, two fragments of which survive in the Gemeentearchief, Haarlem, and the Ian Woodner collection. The latter shows a small circle drawn at the far end of the nave which Saenredam used as the *oog* (eye), or vanishing point, for his composition. A recent measured architectural drawing of the church set against the outlines of the building in the painting shows that Saenredam deliberately distorted the dimensions of the pillars and vault to increase the

sense of monumental grandeur and overwhelming scale.

The picture was probably that mentioned by Constantijn Huyghens as offered to the Stateholder of the United Provinces, Prince Willem II in 1648. Its high quality was certainly recognised as it then seems to have been owned by the burgomaster of Amsterdam, Andries Graeff, from whom it was bought by the States General (The Dutch Republic) to present to King Charles II in England at the Restoration of the monarchy in 1660.

Oil on canvas, 81.1 × 67.8 (arched top)
Presented by William McEwan 1892
NG 827

Rembrandt is the dominant figure of seventeenth-century Dutch art. He was astonishingly inventive in all genres of painting and drawing and his approach to printmaking was groundbreaking. His animated and innovative approach to portraiture (which formed the majority of his commissions) was significantly affected by his prime passion, that of history painting (including biblical and mythological scenes). His work influenced generations of artists, including seventeenth-century contemporaries and twentieth-century painters such as Picasso.

The model for this painting has sometimes been identified as Rembrandt's wife Saskia van Uylenburgh who died in 1642, or as Hendrickje Stoffels, Rembrandt's maid and later his mistress, who was not mentioned as being in the household before 1649. However, the style of the picture suggests it was painted about 1645. If the model for the picture did come from Rembrandt's circle, she is more likely to have been Geertje Dircx, a widow who lived with Rembrandt (c.1643–9) and was nursemaid to his son Titus. Rembrandt gave her Saskia's rings and Geertje sued him for breach of promise when he failed to marry her. Hendrickje testified to Rembrandt's good character and the messy court case ended with Geertje's detention in Gouda. Many of the female figures in Rembrandt's paintings seem to resemble his wife or mistress, but few were probably intended specifically as portraits as he seems to have used the women in his household simply as convenient models for his historical, mythological or biblical scenes.

The raking light and dramatic pose are used to emphasise the impact of illusion, or *trompe l'œil*, in this painting while the gilded headdress and rich bedding may be clues to the narrative. The picture may illustrate a tale from the *Apocrypha*: Sarah watching as her bridegroom Tobias vanquishes the demon who has killed her previous seven husbands on their wedding nights ('*Tobit*', VIII: 1–4). The composition is closely related to Pieter Lastman's painting of the same subject (Boston Museum of Fine Arts). Whoever she is intended to be, the half-dressed woman, poised between anxiety and eagerness, retains a mystery which continues to intrigue.

Rembrandt van Rijn 1606–1669 · Ecce Homo: Christ Presented to the People

Drypoint, 38.3 × 45.5
Accepted in lieu and
allocated through the
National Art Collections
Fund 1992

Unlike Rubens who commissioned other printmakers to follow his designs, Rembrandt produced a whole lifetime's worth of prints which he designed and made himself. It is quite clear that Rembrandt felt passionately about printmaking, experimenting with different techniques and varieties of paper to achieve his desired effect. He would frequently revisit the copper plate after pulling impressions – etching, engraving or scratching-in drypoint lines, sometimes substantially altering the composition in the process. Sometimes prompted by deterioration of the plate through printing, these reworkings, called states, could also give Rembrandt a chance to correct and perfect his designs, as well as potentially increasing sales as collectors sought successive states of a print in order to have the whole 'set'.

This print (here in its fifth state) depicts Pontius Pilate offering the people the chance to free Christ. They choose to release Barabbas instead, ensuring Christ's crucifixion (Matthew 27:15–26). This composition shows a jeering crowd in front of the platform as statues of Justice and Prudence look down from above. Rembrandt was influenced by the 1510 print by Lucas van Leiden of this subject, an impression of which he bought in 1637, part of his extensive art collection. But he later significantly reworked this plate, removing the rabble and replacing them with two arches below the dais, which increases the monumentality of the composition and forces the focus upon the central group with Christ bound before us and left to face his fate. Rembrandt finally dated the seventh state of this print in 1655 but had obviously started work on it before then. It may have been intended as a sort of pendant to one of Rembrandt's most famous prints *The Three Crosses*, also in drypoint and dated 1653 but subsequently dramatically reworked.

Rembrandt van Rijn 1606–1669 · *Self-portrait aged 51* · 165(7?)

Oil on canvas, 53 × 44
Lent by the Duke of Sutherland 1945

No other great artist has portrayed himself so often and in so many ways as Rembrandt. More than eighty paintings and etchings (and a few drawings) made throughout his career seem to chart the course of his life through his face. The date of this striking picture is usually interpreted as 1657 though some think it dates from 1659. The last years of the 1650s were traumatic ones for Rembrandt whose finances were foundering, despite his previous success as one of Amsterdam's most celebrated artists. In 1656, he was forced to seek a *cessio bonorum*, a declaration of legal insolvency. All his property and possessions, including his large art collection, were required to be sold to raise money for his creditors in 1658. Subsequently, a legal arrangement meant that his son Titus and his mistress Hendrickje Stoffels officially ran his business, providing Rembrandt with lodging and upkeep in return for the paintings he continued to produce.

This portrait has a remarkable immediacy. This is partly due to Rembrandt's direct gaze, but also to the way the artist has placed himself up close against the surface of the canvas, leaving very little space surrounding the dominant head. The painstaking handling of paint in the soft surface of the velvet beret and the fine furrowing of wrinkles across the face is somewhat unusual in Rembrandt's work at the time, but such verisimilitude gives an extraordinary impression of being 'face-to-face' with the artist.

Johannes (Jan) Vermeer 1632–1675 · Christ in the House of Martha and Mary

Only about thirty paintings are known by the great Delft artist, renowned for his exquisite interiors of Dutch life. This may be Vermeer's earliest surviving work, probably painted between 1654 and 1655, and is certainly his largest. Though he painted an *Allegory of Faith* (Metropolitan Museum, New York) in the early 1670s, the Edinburgh painting is Vermeer's only known biblical subject. The story comes from the Gospel of St Luke (10:38–42) in which Christ praises Mary's eagerness to sit listening to his teachings, in contrast to her sister Martha's bustling hospitality. The unusual size and subject-matter make it likely the work was specifically commissioned. Only a handful of paintings, apart from this picture, provide any clue to Vermeer's early artistic development. *Diana and her Nymphs*, now in the Mauritshuis, The Hague, is also datable to about 1655 and is similarly unique in Vermeer's oeuvre in being his only mythological subject. This, together with 'The Procuress' (signed and dated 1656) at the Gemäldegalerie, Dresden, and a controversial painting *St Praxedis* (private collection) are the only other suggested early works. Intriguingly, there are no known drawings or studies by the artist.

The composition has little to do with contemporary painting in Delft and Vermeer probably looked elsewhere for inspiration. He may have travelled outside Delft and certainly inherited his father's art dealing business in 1652 which presumably made him familiar with a much wider range of work from artists further afield. No exact prototype has been found for this painting but the most obvious influence upon its broad handling, large scale and religious

nature comes from artists who had travelled to Rome from the Catholic city of Utrecht. They became influenced by the art of Caravaggio (termed the Utrecht Caravaggists), particularly Hendrick ter Brugghen and Abraham Bloemaert, the latter was a distant relative of Vermeer by marriage. This picture was cleverly used by the famous Dutch forger, Hans van Meegeren, in the 1930s as the basis for his forgeries of Vermeer's 'missing' early works, such as the *Christ at Emmaus* (Boijmans van Beuningen Museum, Rotterdam).

Oil on canvas,
158.5 × 141.5
Presented by the sons of
W.A. Coats in memory of
their father 1927
NG 1670

Jacob van Ruisdael 1628/9–1682
The Banks of a River 1649

Oil on canvas, 134 × 193
Sir James Erskine of Torrie
Bequest to the University of
Edinburgh 1835, deposited
on loan 1845 with the
Royal Institution; loan
transferred to the National
Gallery 1859

One of the most important Dutch
landscape artists in the latter half of
the seventeenth century, Ruisdael was
a painter, etcher and draughtsman.
Brought up in Haarlem, he probably
trained with his uncle Salomon van
Ruysdael. However, he rejected the
virtually monotone landscapes
developed by Salomon and artists such
as Jan van Goyen in favour of more
naturalistic compositions and more
lifelike colours; painting mountains,
woodland, dunes, seascapes and
winter scenes.

The Banks of a River, signed and
dated the year after Ruisdael became a
guild master, is adapted from a
painting Ruisdael made earlier in
1647, *River Landscape with a High Sandy
Bank*, now in the Hage Collection,
Nivaagaard, Denmark. However, the
dramatic high sky and extensive
panorama give this picture a grandeur

unmatched by the earlier work.
Ruisdael used drawings of Rhenen on
the Neder Rijn as the inspiration for
the town in the background, and the
tower of the church of St Cunera and
twin towers of Rhenen's watergate can
be seen in the distance. He also
adapted various motifs from the work
of Cornelis Vroom. The figures were
probably not painted by Ruisdael but
perhaps by his friend, Nicolaes
Berchem, or possibly Philips
Wouverman. Such collaboration
between artists was not uncommon,
each bringing their own specialist
skills to the painting.

Willem van de Velde the Elder 1611–1693
A Sea-piece with a Dutch Merchant Ship and a Swedish Flute

The prosperity and independence of the Dutch Republic was predominantly founded on the success of its navy, its fishing fleets and the East and West India trading companies. The desire to celebrate this success gave marine painting a special place in Dutch art. The son of a naval captain, Van de Velde's preoccupation with sea views was probably prompted by his own voyages. Though he was successful in his own right, it was his collaboration with his son Willem that brought Van de Velde most fame, his drawings serving as models for his son's paintings. They emigrated to England in 1672 to work for Charles II, and together they were hailed as the finest marine artists in Europe.

Painted c.1650, this picture shows a large merchant ship, seen from the right bow, with a Dutch flag at the main mast. Close by is an armed *fluit* (or flute: a small war vessel) which flies the Swedish flag. The port in the distance may be West Terschelling. Many of Van de Velde's study drawings were made from direct observation from his own boat, sometimes a dangerous undertaking as he sketched in the midst of sea battles. This detailed technique of 'pen-painting', infinitely more durable than a drawing, was introduced by Hendrick Goltzius but perfected by Van de Velde. The matt background may have been an emulsion of oil and egg, more receptive than oil paint to the water-based black with which the artist drew.

Pen and brush on panel,
60.5 × 83.6
Presented by Hew Hamilton
Dalrymple 1906
NG 933

Gerard ter Borch 1617–1681 · A Singing Practice

Oil on canvas, 73.8 × 79.6
Lent by the Duke of
Sutherland 1945

In the early 1650s, Ter Borch was one of the first artists to contribute to the development of a new simplified genre painting (depicting scenes of everyday life). Earlier genre subjects had tended to show bustling crowded peasant scenes but Ter Borch's images were more bourgeois than bucolic, restrained in handling and with fewer figures. The design of this composition is one of the earliest examples of Ter Borch's mature style. The prime version (c.1654–5) is in the Rijksmuseum, Amsterdam, and a third is in the Gemäldegalerie, Berlin, but only the Sutherland painting shows the girl holding a sheet of music.

The precise subject has long been a cause for debate, an ambiguity perhaps intentionally sought by the artist, who intriguingly keeps the face of the girl concealed. It has usually been stated that the officer in the Berlin version held a coin, perhaps pointing to a little polite prostitution, but this part of the picture is very damaged and may have been misread. There is certainly no coin in the Amsterdam and Sutherland versions. The Amsterdam picture was engraved with the sentimentally bowdlerised title of 'L'Instruction Paternelle', or 'Paternal Admonition' as it appeared in English, though it is difficult to imagine the young officer is the girl's father as he looks at her rather more with a suitor's enthusiasm than with fatherly concern. The music sheet may hint at the potential harmony of the match in what remains an elusive and subtle composition.

Aelbert Cuyp 1620–1691 · Landscape with a View of the Valkhof, Nijmegen

Aelbert Cuyp was the most distinguished of a family of Dordrecht painters and one of the leading Dutch landscape artists of the seventeenth century. His first works, painted in a restricted palette, were influenced by Jan van Goyen. However, he later painted richly-coloured pastoral scenes which showed a knowledge of Dutch Italianate artists such as Jan Both with an emphasis on the warm tones of southern sunshine. Painted between 1655 and 1660, this picture shows the Valkhof palace at Nijmegen, associated with the first stand of the Batavians, ancestors of the Dutch, against invaders and, therefore, of great significance as a symbol of plucky Dutch bravery. The palace was built by Emperor Charlemagne on Roman foundations in 777, rebuilt in 1155 by Frederick Barbarossa and demolished by French revolutionary troops in 1795.

The Valkhof stood on high ground above the River Waal, but the terrain has been levelled out in the painting. The composition is related to Cuyp's drawing of the south-west corner of the building (Pierpont Morgan Library, New York), which is topographically more accurate. The picturesque view and the Valkhof's historical associations attracted the interest of many seventeenth-century Dutch artists and it was painted by Van Goyen and Salomon van Ruisdael. Cuyp painted the palace several times – a version at Woburn Abbey shows nearly the same vantage point as the one in this picture.

Oil on canvas, 113 × 165
Purchased with the aid of
the National Art Collections
Fund 1972 (in recognition
of the services of the Earl of
Crawford and Balcarres to
the National Art Collections
Fund and the National
Galleries of Scotland)
NG 2314

Jan de Braij (de Bray) 1626/7–1697

**Portrait of a Man
1662**
Oil on panel, 23.5 × 17.4
(oval)
Bequest of Mrs Nisbet
Hamilton Ogilvy of Biel
1921
NG 1500

**Portrait of a Woman
1663**
Oil on panel, 23.5 × 17.4
(oval)
Bequest of Mrs Nisbet
Hamilton Ogilvy of Biel
1921
NG 1501

Portrait of a Boy 1662
Oil on panel, 21.2 × 15.2
(oval)
Bequest of Mrs Nisbet
Hamilton Ogilvy of Biel
1921
NG 1502

Portrait of a Boy 1663
Oil on panel, 21.5 × 15.8
(oval)
Bequest of Mrs Nisbet
Hamilton Ogilvy of Biel
1921
NG 1503

Like Frans Hals, Jan de Braij lived and worked in Haarlem. The restricted palette of subdued colours he uses here is typical of burgher portraits in the city at this date. Son of a successful artist, Salomon, De Braij's earliest picture dates from 1651 and he was warden of the Haarlem guild by 1667. He was renowned as a portrait painter but was also commissioned to paint large history pictures and mythological scenes.

Few such groups of family portraits have survived though they must once have been common. These were painted in pairs, the man aged forty-seven with his eldest son aged eleven in 1662 and then the following year, the woman (presumably the man's wife and children's mother) completed when she, too, was forty-seven, with her younger son aged seven. The reason for this gap is unknown but nonetheless, the portraits must have been intended as a set from the outstart. They were probably painted on rectangular panels which were then shaped into ovals, to fit their fine matching seventeenth-century Dutch frames.

Philips Koninck 1619–1688 · *Extensive Landscape* 1666

Oil on canvas, 91 × 111.8
Purchased by Private Treaty
1986
NG 2434

The panorama had been a popular form of landscape in the Low Countries since Pieter Bruegel the Elder (c.1525–1569), but Koninck gave a new quality to this form, combining imaginary majestic views with more naturalistic vistas. Unlike the distinctive views over the flat dunes surrounding Haarlem that Jacob van Ruisdael perfected, Koninck's landscapes are less rooted in topographical accuracy but manage, nonetheless, through their low horizons and large skies, to convey the spirit of the wide Dutch plains.

Philips Koninck was born in Amsterdam and was related to a family of goldsmiths and painters. He was apprenticed to his brother Jacob in Rotterdam for about three years from 1637. There he met his wife, the daughter of a Rotterdam surgeon, whom he married in 1641. Her brother was Abraham Furnerius, a pupil of Rembrandt. Philips's art was noticeably influenced by Rembrandt but there is no proof that he joined Rembrandt's studio when he returned to Amsterdam in 1642. Being of independent means through his second marriage, Koninck could afford to concentrate on these broad vistas with their high viewpoint whose details evoked his native Gelderland, and he painted this sort of landscape almost exclusively. He appears to have stopped painting in about 1676 but his reputation was sufficiently high for his self-portrait of 1667 to be bought by Cosimo III de' Medici for the Artists' Gallery in the Uffizi, Florence, where it still hangs.

Meindert Hobbema 1638–1709 · *Wooded Landscape*

Oil on canvas,
93.7 × 130.8
Purchased with the aid of
the National Art Collections
Fund and the National
Heritage Purchase Grant
(Scotland) 1979
NG 2377

Hobbema is often considered the last of the great seventeenth-century Dutch landscape painters. He was christened Meindert Lubbertsz. in Amsterdam but adopted the surname Hobbema in his youth. He trained with Jacob van Ruisdael (c.1658–60), and though his earliest works seem to emulate the work of his master's uncle Salomon, his painting owed a profound debt to Jacob, who appears to have been a friend as well as artistic mentor and was a witness to Hobbema's marriage.

This painting is a good example of woodland scenes in which Hobbema specialised, painted in c.1662–3, at a period when Hobbema had begun to strike out on his own, relying less directly on Ruisdael's compositions, using a lighter palette and more delicate technique. Though it seems naturalistic, this view was certainly not made from nature and the apparent spontaneity of the composition is, in fact, carefully constructed with its skilful contrast between the darkened foreground and brightly lit middle distance. The critic, Gustaav Waagen, praised the picture in 1857 for its 'powerful and transparent' effect and the 'cool silvery tones' of the middle ground. Hobbema's work was extremely popular in Britain from the eighteenth century onwards and had a great influence on British landscape painting.

Jan Steen 1625/6–1679 · A School for Boys and Girls

Jan Steen is best known for his genre scenes of rowdy life but he also painted portraits and biblical and mythological scenes.

This is the biggest of several schoolroom scenes by Steen and was painted in about 1670. (Another, less elaborate, composition is in the National Gallery of Ireland, Dublin.) The theme of the unruly school had previously been depicted by both Isack and Adriaen van Ostade. Steen clearly took a certain amount of glee in portraying the evils of inattentiveness in a school without discipline but although Dutch children were often considered unruly and spoilt, contemporary records show that the level of literacy was comparatively high for Europe. Here the pandemonium wrought by the pupils is studiously ignored by the schoolmaster and his wife who make no attempt to regain order. A print of Hans Holbein's portrait of the great scholar Erasmus of Rotterdam is pointedly discarded under the bench at the right. A small boy offers a pair of spectacles to the owl perched near a lamp, acting out a Dutch proverb: 'What use are glasses or light if the owl does not want to see?' (similar to the saying 'You can lead a horse to water...'). Ironically, the owl was also a symbol of wisdom, the attribute of the goddess Athena. Continuing such learned allusions, Steen loosely based the whole of the design for his picture on Raphael's composition of the *School of Athens (La Disputa)* in the Vatican. It is part of the artist's intelligent joke to base this classroom chaos on the dignified grouping of the greatest scholars of antiquity.

Oil on canvas,
81.7 × 108.6
Purchased by Private Treaty with the aid of the National Heritage Memorial Fund 1984
NG 2421

Jan Weenix c.1642–1719 · Landscape with a Huntsman and Dead Game ('Allegory of the Sense of Smell') 1697

Oil on canvas, 344 × 323
Purchased 1990
NG 2523

This picture is the largest of a series of five paintings that Weenix painted as an immensely grand decorative scheme, probably commissioned for a house built by a wealthy Portuguese Jew, at 99 Nieuwe Herengracht in Amsterdam. Archives relating to the house in the early eighteenth century mention the 'fixed paintings', almost certainly these canvases which were set into panels in the lavish first-floor salon. The pictures are allegories of the five senses. In this work the dogs at the right and left of the picture symbolise the sense of smell. Three of the other four pictures are still known. The *Allegory of Hearing* (depicted by musicians in an architectural setting) is at the Allen Museum, Oberlin, Ohio, while *Taste* and *Sight* both now hang in a New York hotel. The whole set was bought from Amsterdam in the 1920s by the press magnate, William Randolph Hearst (on whom the film *Citizen Kane* was based). This painting was sold to RKO and later to Paramount studios and appears as a backdrop in a Bob Hope movie of 1946.

The son and pupil of the artist Jan Baptist Weenix, Jan's earliest paintings resemble his father's Italianate work to such an extent that they are almost indistinguishable, but he developed a more refined style after his father's death (c.1660/1). Jan was renowned for his game pieces and his opulent, striking style was popular with the nobility. He worked for the Elector Palatine from 1702 to 1714, creating a magnificent series of twelve huge canvases for the elector's hunting lodge at the Schloss Bensberg (fragments are now at the Alte Pinakothek, Munich). However, this 1697 series of *Allegories* is one of his earliest attempts at such a decorative scheme. It is even possible that the unusual scale and evident success of this work was in some way instrumental in the award of the Bensburg commission. It proved him supremely capable of painting impressive still life, figures, flowers, landscape and statuary, while the others in the series clearly demonstrated his ability in portraying children, seascapes and architecture, thereby displaying Weenix's impressive range of artistic talent.

Albrecht Dürer 1471–1528 · The Four Horsemen of the Apocalypse
from The Apocalypse: Revelation of Saint John the Divine

Woodcut on paper,
39.2 × 28.2
(to edge of block)
1511 edition
Purchased 1965

Dürer produced religious paintings, portraits, drawings, ornamental designs, and treatises on fortification and proportion, but his reputation as a printmaker outshone all of these. The quality and sheer invention of his designs for woodcuts and engravings raised the status of printmaking as an art, and his prints were collected and copied throughout Europe. Born in prosperous Nuremberg, he was the son of a goldsmith but was apprenticed to Michael Wolgemut, a painter and woodcut designer, from 1486 to 1489. Dürer spent a productive time travelling from 1490 to 1495, his journey to Italy perhaps encouraged by his circle of Humanist friends.

Made in 1498, this is one of the most famous examples of northern printmaking, a technical tour de force and a masterpiece of composition. St John's vision reveals four terrible harbingers of destruction. Relentless and remorseless, they trample all before them. Furthest away from us we see Death the Conqueror, next to him War, then Famine, then the shrivelled Reaper, pitching his felled harvest into the mouth of Hell. Dürer made sixteen innovatory large-format woodcuts to illustrate the New Testament Book of Revelation (the first such work in Western art to be published and illustrated by an artist), influenced his godfather Anton Koberger's Bible first printed in 1483. The subject was frequently illustrated, particularly just before 1500, when many believed the world would end. Dürer himself depicted an apocalyptic comet on the reverse of his little panel of St Jerome painted in the late 1490s (now in the National Gallery, London).

Hans Krafft the Elder 1481–1542
Dedication Medal of the City of Nuremberg for Emperor Charles V, 1521

This elaborate, and technically superb, silver medal was designed by Albrecht Dürer, his only known design for one of the most celebrated medals of the German Renaissance. The medal was exquisitely made by Hans Krafft who had trained as a goldsmith and worked for Frederick the Wise of Saxony and later for the municipal mint of his native Nuremberg.

The front (*obverse*) shows the young Habsburg emperor wearing the Order of the Golden Fleece while the reverse has the coat of arms of his new dominions above a letter 'N' for Nuremberg. Charles was elected to succeed his grandfather Maximilian I as emperor, and was crowned in Aachen in 1520. It was traditional for the new emperor to convene his first parliament (*Diet*) in Nuremberg so the city council commissioned Dürer, the city's most famous artist, to design a commemorative medal, 100 of which were to be presented to Charles V. But plague struck Nuremberg in 1521 and the *Diet* convened in Worms instead, so the completed medals with the now irrelevant armorial references to Nuremberg were never presented. Fewer than ten copies of the medal survive today, though 167 medals were made – most were melted down in 1537. Dürer attended Charles V's coronation during his stay in the Netherlands (1520–1) and mentioned this medal in the diary he kept of his journey.

Obverse
Charles V (1500–1558) Holy Roman Emperor
Reverse
The double-headed eagle of the Holy Roman Empire with the arms of Austria and Burgundy
Silver, 7.2 diameter
Purchased 1993
NG 2566

Franconian Master active c.1515
The Lamentation of Christ with a Group of Donors

Oil on panel, 120.5 × 97
Purchased with the aid of
the National Art Collections
Fund 1998
NG 2689

This panel, formerly part of an altarpiece flanked by two wings showing Saints George and Christopher, is by an unknown master working in Franconia in south-western Germany in the first quarter of the sixteenth century. The painter clearly knew the work of Albrecht Dürer (1471–1528) – the greyhound at the foot of the donors' prie-dieu is a direct 'quote' from Dürer's engraving of *Saint Eustace*, c.1501, while the grouping of the figures partially echoes Dürer's painted *Lamentation* from *The Seven Sorrows of the the Virgin*, 1495/6 (now in the Staatliche Museum, Dresden). However, the decorative nature of much of the picture and its rich colouristic effects also call to mind paintings by Lucas Cranach the Elder (1472–1553) and the artist was

perhaps associated with Cranach's industrious Wittenberg workshop in some way.

The bearded donor with a rosary and the kneeling figure wear the elaborate gold insignia of the knightly and religious Order of the Swan (*Schwanenorden*), founded in 1440 by Friedrich II, Elector of Brandenburg. The Order, particularly popular in Franconia, was devoted to the veneration of the Virgin and to the relief of suffering through charity. Its chapel, dedicated to St George, was in the Ansbach church of St Gumbertus.

It has been suggested that this was a memorial for the burial of Margrave Kasimir of Brandenburg-Kulmbach who died in 1527. However, technical research reveals the outside of the wings (now owned by Compton Verney House, Warwickshire) were originally marbled and then later 'upgraded' in 1519 by overpainting female saints on top. The central panel and insides of the wings must therefore have been finished before 1519, perhaps in about 1515. It is not yet known why this might have been done but it is hoped that further research may reveal the donors of this distinctive panel and perhaps, even, the identity of its talented artist.

Hans Holbein the Younger 1497/8–1543
An Allegory of the Old and New Testaments

Born in Augsburg, Holbein was trained by his father and then worked in Basle. He stayed in England from 1526 to 1528, returning to Switzerland, and then settled in England where he lived from 1532 until his death. Holbein was appointed court painter to Henry VIII from 1536, and it is his portraiture of the Tudor court for which he is predominantly remembered today. However, he also painted religious works and designed decorative schemes. This exquisitely painted panel is effectively a visual sermon, clarifying complicated dogma through direct images. It illustrates a central theme of the Reformation: the contrast between the unyielding Old Testament Law (LEX) on the left, and the forgiving New Testament Grace (GRATIA) at the right. The failure of

Man (HOMO) to obey the commandments God gave to Moses, led to sin (PECCATUM) and death (MORS – the skeleton). However, Man is forgiven and achieves salvation (VICTORIA NOSTRA) through the Crucifixion of Christ. Poor naked Man, in a pose recalling Hercules at the crossroads, sits beleaguered by the Old Testament prophet Isaiah, but John the Baptist, 'messenger' of Christ, points to the right spiritual path.

It is not known who commissioned this picture which was probably painted in the early 1530s, but the composition may derive from a design by Lucas Cranach the Elder. Luther and Cranach were friends in Wittenburg, a centre for the development of Reformation symbolism. Holbein may have known this design through prints.

Oil on panel, 50 × 60.5
Purchased by Private Treaty with the aid of the National Heritage Memorial Fund and the National Heritage Purchase Grant (Scotland) 1981
NG 2407

Lucas Cranach the Elder 1472–1553 · *Venus and Cupid*

Oil on panel, 38.1 × 27
Bequest of the 11th Marquess of Lothian 1941
NG 1942

Lucas Cranach was born in Kronach, a Franconian town about fifteen miles from Coburg, under the rule of the Electors of Saxony. Cranach trained there with his father Hans but travelled to Vienna, perhaps as early as 1500–1. He was initially influenced by Dürer's work (who was one year his senior), but rapidly established an independent style, full of vivid invention, and dramatic colour. Employed by Frederick the Wise in Wittenburg from 1505, Cranach continued as court artist to the Electors of Saxony for half a century until his death. He established a prolific workshop by 1507 (later continued by his sons), producing portraits, altarpieces, allegorical and mythological compositions, as well as designs for costume, emblems and weaponry.

Cranach was a close friend of Martin Luther who was godfather to his daughter. However, despite his allegiance to the Protestant reformer, he became fascinated with portraying the nude from about 1520. Inspired by Renaissance secularity but without classical examples to follow, Cranach developed his own languid yet naïve nudes, exuding an acceptable courtly eroticism.

This panel is signed with a winged serpent, the motif Cranach adopted as his coat of arms, awarded him by the elector in 1508. From c.1537, the serpent's wings appear folded instead of upright. This was perhaps painted a couple of years later, along with a number of versions (though never copies) of the same subject. Its closest affinity is to a painting in a private collection in Zurich.

Adam Elsheimer 1578–1610 · The Stoning of Saint Stephen

Elsheimer's work, always small in scale and fastidious in execution, had a profound influence on many artists, especially those visiting Rome from Northern Europe. Born and trained in Frankfurt, he travelled via Venice to Rome where he settled. His early death aged thirty-two and his slow working process mean that his work is extremely rare. Despite this, his compositions were widely known, as circulated through prints.

St Stephen was the first Christian martyr, who during his martyrdom saw a vision of the 'heavens opened' with Christ standing by God (Apostles 6–7). A version of this composition is on loan to the Wallraf-Richartz Museum, Cologne. Almost identical in size but with some variations, it demonstrates a similar fascination with oriental costume and thronging crowds, perhaps influenced by the art of Tintoretto which Elsheimer would have seen during his Venetian stay of 1598–1600. The Cologne picture may have been painted in Venice and the magnificent Edinburgh version, far richer in detail and more complicated in composition, was perhaps a re-working of the subject made a few years later in Rome (c.1603–4). It must have been seen there by Rubens c.1608, since a drawing of his, now at the British Museum, London, incorporates many figures from the design. Both versions of Elsheimer's St Stephen may have been owned by the artist Paul Bril.

Oil on tinned copper,
34.7 × 28.6
Purchased 1965
NG 2281

Henry Fuseli (Johann Heinrich Füssli) 1741–1825
Portrait of Mrs Fuseli 1800

Brush and grey wash over traces of black chalk on paper, 22 × 15.4
Purchased by Private Treaty 1987
D 5146

Fuseli was one of the most spirited and original artists to work in Britain at the turn of the eighteenth century. Born in Switzerland, he spent an influential period in Italy before settling in London where, despite being somewhat unorthodox, he was made Professor of Painting at the Royal Academy from 1799 to 1804 and from 1810 to 1825. A self-taught artist, well versed in the classical tradition, Fuseli infused his subjects with an emotional intensity that often created unconventional images of disturbing power.

He depicted women often and obsessively. His wife and other modish models, courtesans, predatory sirens, and heroines such as Lucrezia Borgia and Lady Macbeth were portrayed with a stylistic exaggeration once referred to as 'Sado-Mannerism'. Hair also held a fetishistic fascination for Fuseli and he revelled in drawing complicated coiffure. This drawing of 31 May 1800 represents Sophia Rawlins, from Batheaston village near Bath, whom Fuseli married in 1788. An amateur artist's model, she was much younger than her husband and both socially and intellectually his inferior. However the numerous drawings and paintings Fuseli made of her, mostly in the 1790s, attest that her allure was compelling, and the marriage proved long-lasting.

31 May 1800.

W. Loeillot after Karl Friedrich Schinkel 1781–1841
Design for a Royal Palace at Orianda in the Crimea

Schinkel numbers among Germany's most accomplished and versatile artistic figures. Renowned as a painter of romantic landscapes, as well as a designer of stage sets, interiors, furniture and ornamental objects, he is celebrated, above all, as an outstanding architect, whose buildings, such as the classical styled *Neue Wache* (Guardhouse), *Schauspielhaus* (Royal Theatre) and *Altes Museum* (Old Museum) transformed early nineteenth-century Berlin.

In his architectural designs, Schinkel sought to combine the experiences and forms of the past with contemporary materials and technology. His quest for a modern style found full expression in two ambitious projects for palace complexes on the Acropolis in Athens, and at Orianda on the Crimean coast. Commissioned in the 1830s respectively by King Otto of Greece, and

Alexandra Fedorovna, Tsarina of Russia, Schinkel's elaborate schemes represented the culmination of his life's learning and practice. Sadly, the projects' exorbitant costs deemed both impractical and neither was realised. Schinkel's magnificent presentation drawings and watercolours were reproduced as elegant engravings and brilliant colour lithographs, which were issued in two parts between 1840 and 1848 under the collective title *Werke der höheren Baukunst (Works of higher Architecture)*. The National Gallery of Scotland owns one of the finest sets of these prints. The group boasts an exceptional provenance, having been gifted by King Friedrich Wilhelm IV of Prussia (Schinkel's greatest royal admirer and patron), to the distinguished British antiquarian and diplomat William Richard Hamilton (1779–1859).

Perspective View of the Sea Terrace
Published 1847
Chromolithograph on paper, (platemark) 48 × 49
Purchased with support by the National Lottery through the Heritage Lottery Fund 1997
P 2910.20

Jean Clouet c.1485/90–c.1540/41
Madame de Canaples (Marie d'Assigny, 1502–1558)

Oil on panel, 36 × 28.5
Bequest of the 11th
Marquess of Lothian 1941
NG 1930

Clouet was probably of Flemish origin but spent much of his life working for the court of François I of France where he painted many portraits of the king and his entourage. He is documented first as living at Tours but then evidently established himself in Paris. Despite his apparent eminence during his own day, he was only rediscovered by historians in the middle of the nineteenth century, and even then much confusion remained, to the extent that the majority of French sixteenth-century portraits were once loosely attributed to 'Clouet'. A further complication was the presence of Jean's son François, who succeeded to his father's position at court and whose painting style was remarkably similar. Both men were known by the nickname of 'Janet'.

The identification of the subject of this portrait is based on a drawing by Clouet at Chantilly in which the inscription identifies the sitter as Madame de Canaples. She was a lady at the court of François I and was born Marie (or Judith) d'Assigny. In 1525, the probable date of this portrait, she married Jean de Créqui, sire de Canaples. In portraits such as this Clouet continued the French tradition, while borrowing elements from both Italian and Flemish art.

Guillaume Dupré c.1579–1640
Francesco IV de Gonzaga, Duke of Mantua (1586–1612)

The Latin inscription states 'Francesco IV, by the grace of God, fifth Duke of Mantua, third Duke of Monferrat, the first year of his reign, aged 26'. This medal was made to celebrate his accession in February 1612 but Francesco died of smallpox in December of that year. Also painted by Rubens in Mantua a few years earlier (in a fragment now in the Kunsthistorisches Museum, Vienna), the duke is here shown wearing the collar of the Order of the Precious Blood of Our Saviour. This had been founded by his father Vincenzo IV Gonzaga in 1608, in honour of Francesco's marriage to Princess Margharita of Savoy. The insignia of the Order (which lapsed in 1708) was a phial of Christ's blood flanked by two angels.

Dupré was probably summoned from France to Italy to make this medal. The Mantuan court had strong links with France as Francesco's mother was the favourite sister of Marie de Medici and godmother of Louis XIII. The choice of Dupré suggests the high status of the Gonzagas, for Dupré was the greatest of all French medallists. Probably trained by the sculptor Barthélemey Prieur (whose daughter he married), Dupré became 'Controller General' of sculpture at the French Mint in 1604 and first sculptor to the king in 1611. This medal is of exceptional quality (perhaps intended to outshine all Italian competition) and is a superlative example of court portrait sculpture in miniature.

Bronze uniface medal, 16.8 (diameter)
Purchased with the aid of the National Art Collections Fund 1989
NG 2504

Nicolas Poussin 1594–1665 · The Mystic Marriage of Saint Catherine

Oil on panel, 126 × 168
Bequest of Sir John
Heathcoat Amory 1973
NG 2319

Poussin has always been regarded as one of the most learned of all visual artists and is rightly considered the founder of the classical tradition in French painting. He was born in Les Andelys in Normandy. After fairly obscure artistic beginnings in Paris, he arrived in Rome in 1624 where he remained for the rest of his life except for a brief and unhappy return to Paris (1640–2). In his first years in Rome Poussin's art displayed a sensuous quality which would later be replaced by an increasingly stern classicism. This early picture of 1628–9 is, very unusually, painted on five oak panels, canvas being the normal support for paintings made in Italy at that time. It depicts the early Christian Saint Catherine of Alexandria (supposedly fourth century) who, after having been baptised by a hermit, refused marriage to the emperor and was accepted by the infant Christ as His bride. She was later martyred by first being broken on a wheel (after which is named the firework 'Catherine Wheel') and then beheaded. The painting belonged to Cassiano dal Pozzo (1588–1657), the great antiquarian and collector who was employed by the Barberini family. He was the most important of Poussin's patrons in Rome and commissioned from him the first of the two great sets of the seven Sacraments. Bernini's marble bust of Cassiano's uncle, Carlo Antonio dal Pozzo (see p.48), is now in the collection of the National Gallery of Scotland.

Nicolas Poussin 1594–1665 · A Dance to the Music of Time

Poussin regarded drawing primarily as a means to an end. Most of his existing studies were made in preparation for paintings, rather than as finished works in their own right. Lightly squared for enlargement, this composition is the only surviving drawing for Poussin's painting *A Dance to the Music of Time* (Wallace Collection, London). Commissioned by Cardinal Guilio Rospigliosi (later Pope Clement IX), the painting is generally thought to have been executed between 1637 and 1640 (although a date of 1632–4 has also been proposed in recent years). The title by which the painting is now known originated in the twentieth century, and was adopted by the English author Anthony Powell (1905–2000) for his famous twelve-volume series of novels of the same name.

According to Bellori (Poussin's first biographer) the work's subject was dictated by its patron. Interpreted as an allegory of man's fortune, the dancers personify poverty, labour,

riches and pleasure, their wheeling motion representing the perpetual cycle of human life. Their dance is performed to the lyre of Father Time. Two putti play with Time's hourglass and blow soap bubbles, both emblems of life's brevity. The two-headed Janus term, with an old head looking back and a young head looking forward, refers to time's passage, while in the sky the sun, preceded by dawn, drives his chariot through the ring of the zodiac. In the finished painting, which differs in several significant details, the strong shadows and rhythmic vigour of the drawing are replaced by a cool morning light and a more sedate sense of movement.

Pen and brown ink and wash on paper; traces of squaring in black chalk, 14.8 × 19.9
Purchased by Private Treaty, with the aid of the National Art Collections Fund (Scottish Fund), the Pilgrim Trust, the Edith M. Ferguson Bequest and contributions from two private donors 1984
D 5127

Nicolas Poussin 1594–1665 · The Sacrament of Ordination

Oil on canvas, 117 × 178
Lent by the Duke of
Sutherland 1945

Sacrament is the Latin equivalent of the Greek for 'mystery' and many of the early Christian writers drew parallels between the mysteries of Greek religion and the Sacraments or rites of Christianity. Comparative religion was of great interest to the intellectual circles in which Poussin moved in Rome. He painted two series of the seven Sacraments. The first was for Cassiano dal Pozzo and was begun in the 1630s and completed by 1642. The second, and arguably greater, series was executed between 1644 and 1648 for Poussin's friend and patron Paul Fréart de Chantelou who, in 1645, was appointed secretary in Paris to the Duc d'Enghien. It is this series which is now on loan to the National Gallery of Scotland. The Sacraments were rarely represented in art, especially in southern Europe, and Poussin was the first artist to attempt to display them in their true historical setting, that is in the Rome of the early Christian church. In this painting, despatched to Chantelou on 19 August 1647, Christ gives the 'keys of heaven' (Matthew 16:16–19) to Peter, the Prince of Apostles. The large 'E' on the column on the left may refer to Ecclesia, the foundation of the Roman Church on Peter; or to the mysterious 'E' at the sanctuary of Apollo at Delphi. Christian and pagan philosophy were equally rich sources of subject-matter for Poussin.

Nicolas Poussin 1594–1665 · The Sacrament of Extreme Unction

In order to illustrate this Sacrament of final blessing Poussin depicts in a very moving fashion the death scene of a Christian Roman soldier who is anointed with holy oil by a priest. On the back wall is a shield with the Chi-rho, the monogram of Christ, denoting the dead man is a 'soldier of Christ'. The scene owes much in its design to classical funerary reliefs. The figures are arranged as though on a stage set with centralised perspective, and it is known from descriptions by his contemporaries that Poussin used a model stage when working out a composition involving a number of figures. When Bernini, the great Italian architect and sculptor, saw the second set of Sacraments in Chantelou's Parisian residence in 1665, he studied them for an hour. He then got down on his knees, changed his spectacles and finally said 'You have shown me the merit of an artist who makes me realise I am nothing.'

Oil on canvas, 117 × 178
Lent by the Duke of
Sutherland 1945

Claude Lorrain 1600/5–1682
Landscape with Apollo and the Muses 1652

Oil on canvas, 186 × 290
Purchased with the aid of
the National Art Collections
Fund and a Treasury Grant
1960
NG 2240

Claude Gellée (as he was originally known) came from the duchy of Lorraine and was called 'Le Lorrain'. An early biography states he trained as a pastry cook. He spent most of his long career based in Rome and is generally considered to be the founder of classical landscape painting, that is idealised landscape which, though based on observation of nature, was carefully composed in the studio. Such landscapes were intended to evoke the world of antiquity and were used as settings for both classical and biblical narratives. Claude's ideal landscapes were bought both by patrons in Rome and throughout Europe. They were also very popular with British Grand Tourists in the eighteenth century, who bought them from Italian collections and often had the parks of their country houses designed in imitation of Claude's painted landscapes.

This is Claude's largest and most ambitious landscape and was painted in Rome for Cardinal Pamphili. Its subject is the god Apollo who, surrounded by the nine muses, plays his lyre as four mortals approach to listen. They are placed on the wooded slopes of Mount Helicon. Above them the winged horse Pegasus stands over the spring called Hippocrene. In purely visual terms, however, the real subject of this picture is the breathtakingly beautiful landscape which extends to the horizon.

Gaspard Dughet, called Gaspard Poussin 1615–1675
Classical Landscape with a Lake

Born in Rome, Gaspard was a pupil of Nicolas Poussin, whose sister he married and whose surname he adopted. His work combines aspects of the landscapes of his great contemporaries, Poussin and Claude Lorrain, though Gaspard rarely included human figures for anything more than decorative effect; his landscapes contain few narratives. On occasion he favoured a wilder, rougher kind of nature than Claude or Poussin. His paintings proved extremely popular with British Grand Tourists in the eighteenth century who brought them back from Italy to decorate their town and country houses, often placing them over doorways. His work was highly influential on a number of artists, notably the Welsh landscape painter Richard Wilson, and he was also highly regarded by the theorists and landscape gardeners of the Picturesque movement in the latter half of the eighteenth century. The dating of Gaspard's landscapes is problematic and this exceptionally beautiful example of his work has been variously dated between the 1640s and 1660s. The attribution to Gaspard, which there seems no good reason to doubt, is on grounds of style, though it has recently been proposed that the picture may be by Nicolas Poussin. The most probable solution is that this is a late work by Gaspard but heavily influenced by the classical balance of composition Nicolas Poussin achieved in his own landscapes.

Oil on canvas, 73 × 99
Purchased 1973
NG 2318

Jean-Antoine Watteau 1684–1721 · *Fêtes Vénitiennes*

Oil on canvas, 55.9 × 45.7
Bequest of Lady Murray of
Henderland 1861
NG 439

Born in Valenciennes, Watteau was often considered by his contemporaries to be a Flemish painter. His training and subsequent career in Paris, allied to the delicate sophistication of his art, place him firmly in the French school however. One of the key figures of the Rococo, his work is distinguished by its fragile delicacy permeated by an underlying melancholy. He specialised in the painting of so-called fêtes galantes – scenes in which exquisitely dressed young people idle away time in dreamy, romantic, pastoral settings. The ancestry of such imagery ultimately leads back to the concept of the Garden of Love.

This is one of the greatest of all Watteau's compositions and was probably painted c.1718–19. There may be an autobiographical element. The male dancer on the left is undoubtedly the Flemish painter Nicolas Vleughels with whom Watteau lodged (1718–19); the sickly-looking musette player on the right is Watteau himself, while the dancer may be the actress Charlotte Desmares. It is, therefore, possible that the picture contains a private meaning. The title by which it is generally known, *Fêtes Vénitiennes*, is that used in an engraving after it by L. Cars which was published in 1732.

Jean-Siméon Chardin 1699–1779 · *A Vase of Flowers*

One of the greatest of all still-life painters, Chardin occupied an unusual position in the complex hierarchy of French eighteenth-century art. In 1728 he was received into the French Académie as a painter of 'animals and fruit' and from the mid-1750s until near the end of his life he was responsible for the organising and hanging of the exhibitions of the Académie at the Paris Salon. Extremely popular with contemporary collectors and hailed by the foremost art critic of his day, Denis Diderot, as a 'great magician, with your silent compositions!', Chardin suffered posthumous neglect. His unassuming art was seemingly incompatible with the stern morality and complex figurative compositions of Neoclassicism, the style which dominated French art at the end of the eighteenth and beginning of the nineteenth century. It was only towards the middle of the nineteenth century that he was rediscovered by Realist critics such as Théophile Thoré (who was also the principal agent in the 'rediscovery' of Vermeer around this time), and subsequently influenced a whole host of Realist still-life painters. Chardin's scenes of everyday life (of which fine examples can be found in the Hunterian Art Gallery, University of Glasgow) had a profound effect on such major nineteenth-century artists as Millet and Courbet.

This is Chardin's only surviving flower-piece and probably dates from the mid-1750s. One of the best-known of all his works, it depicts a Delft vase in which are arranged flowers which have been identified as red and white carnations, tube-roses, sweet peas, crocuses and lilies.

Oil on canvas, 45.2 × 37.1
Purchased 1937
NG 1883

Jean-Baptiste Greuze 1725–1805 · A Boy with a Lesson-book

Oil on canvas, 62.5 × 49
Bequest of Lady Murray of
Henderland 1861
NG 436

Greuze enjoyed great popularity in the period between the Rococo and Neo-classicism as a painter of sentimental and melodramatic genre scenes, that is, scenes of everyday life. Their moralising content attracted the admiration of the critics, most notably Denis Diderot. Greuze's attempt to translate his morality tales into the sterner world of neoclassical history painting were less successful, however. He ceased to exhibit at the Paris Salon after he was accepted into the French Académie in 1769 only as a genre, rather than as a history painter.

Greuze was in Italy from 1755 to 1757 and apparently executed this picture at the end of his stay there, exhibiting it back in Paris at the 1757 Salon. It depicts a boy committing a text to memory, his hand placed over the book he is memorising. His unusual coiffure, with the hair pulled up into a central braid, was probably adapted from that found in a marble bust by Jacques Saly of his own daughter, exhibited at the 1750 Salon and known in many versions. Although painted in Italy, this moving picture, a study in concentration, shows the strong influence of Dutch seventeenth-century painting and, in its subtle brown tonalities, of Rembrandt in particular.

Jean-Baptiste Greuze 1725–1805 · A Girl with a Dead Canary

This is the second, and most celebrated, of Greuze's treatments of this subject, which was of a type which held an immense appeal for French eighteenth-century audiences with their predilection for scenes that played on the emotions. It was exhibited at the 1765 Paris Salon where it attracted great critical attention, most famously in the critic Denis Diderot's long commentary in which he created an imaginary conversation with the heartbroken girl. According to Diderot's fanciful interpretation, the girl had recently been visited, in her mother's absence, by her lover. In her distraction afterwards she had unintentionally permitted her bird, a gift from her lover, to die of starvation. Grief-stricken, she weeps over the bird's death and also at the possibility of abandonment by her lover. A more prosaic, but perhaps more plausible, explanation has been advanced in recent scholarship, whereby the picture illustrates a poem by the Roman poet Catullus which Greuze could have known in translation and which describes a young girl's first confrontation with the mystery of death:

'The sparrow's dead, my girl's own sparrow
That she loved more than her eyes.'

This picture was extremely popular in the eighteenth century and was copied many times by other artists.

Oil on canvas, 53.3 × 46 (oval)
Bequest of Lady Murray of Henderland 1861
NG 435

Louis Gauffier 1761–1801 · *Cleopatra and Octavian*

Oil on canvas,
83.8 × 112.5
*Purchased with the aid of
the National Art Collections
Fund 1991*
NG 2526

Born at Poitiers, Gauffier studied in Paris and was joint winner in 1784 of the Prix de Rome. In 1793 he was forced by anti-French feeling to leave Rome for Florence where he concentrated on portraiture and conversation pieces as well as taking an increasing interest in landscape painting. He died at Livorno en route for Paris.

This picture was commissioned in 1787 by the Comte d'Angiviller as a pendant or pair to the reduction he already owned of David's *Belisarius*. It depicts the episode described in Plutarch's *Lives* in which Octavian, after he has defeated Antony at the Battle of Actium in 31 BC, visits the Egyptian queen Cleopatra who, seductively but unsuccessfully, attempts to convince him of her innocence and remorse for the part she played in opposing him. Un-

moved, Octavian rejects all her excuses. Cleopatra then directs Octavian's attention to his great-uncle Julius Caesar, reading from the tender letters she had received from him and pointing out the portraits of him she has displayed in her room.

This picture, which was much admired when it was displayed at the French Académie in Rome in 1788, is a relatively early example of the European enthusiasm for a revival of interest in the art and culture of ancient Egypt.

Jean-Victor Bertin 1767–1842 · *Classical Landscape* 1800

A pupil of the father of neoclassical landscape painting, Pierre-Henri de Valenciennes, Bertin was a regular exhibitor at the Paris Salon from 1793 until his death. He was instrumental in the establishment in 1817 of a competition held every four years for the Prix de Rome for Historical Landscape Painting: this marked an important step in the emancipation of landscape painting as a separate category in French art. Camille Corot, now considered one of the most important forerunners of Impressionism, was one of Bertin's many pupils.

Classical Landscape was shown by Bertin at the 1800 Salon in Paris. It is a typical, highly finished landscape of the period, greatly influenced by the example of seventeenth-century landscape painters such as Claude Lorrain and Nicolas Poussin. Neo-

classical landscape presented nature in idealised form, as it ought to be rather than as it was, recalling the world of classical antiquity which inspired such visions. Here two shepherds make an offering to a term of Pan set beneath trees, while to the left two female figures handle garlands of flowers.

Oil on canvas, 63.5 × 87
Purchased 1988
NG 2465

François, Baron Gérard 1770–1837
Mary Nisbet, Countess of Elgin (1777–1855)

Oil on canvas, 64.8 × 54.6
Bequest of Mrs Nisbet
Hamilton Ogilvy of Biel
1921
NG 1496

Born in Rome, Gérard entered the studio of the great neoclassical painter Jacques-Louis David in 1786. He later became Napoleon's favourite portrait painter and portrayed many members of the emperor's family. He also painted a subject from Ossian for Napoleon at his château at Malmaison. Gérard enjoyed great success as a history painter during both the First Empire and restoration and received many honours during his lifetime, being created Baron in 1819. The subject of this portrait, Mary Nisbet of Dirleton, married Thomas Bruce

(1766–1841), 7th Earl of Elgin, in 1799. They divorced in 1808. This portrait of her may have been painted by Gérard in Paris, possibly just before Elgin, at that time British Ambassador to France, was imprisoned at Lourdes following Napoleon's revocation of the Treaty of Amiens in 1803. Mary interceded with Napoleon on her husband's behalf and Elgin was placed on parole at Pau. Elgin evidently kept this portrait of his wife with him during his confinement. According to Mary, 'it was done by the best painter here, and he took uncommon pains about it'.

François, Baron Gérard 1770–1837
Madame Mère (Maria Laetitia Ramolino Bonaparte, 1750–1836)

Napoleon's mother, who became known as Madame Mère, was born in Ajaccio, Corsica, to a family of Tuscan origin. She married in 1764 Charles-Marie Bonaparte, a lawyer who had trained in Pisa. They had thirteen children of whom eight survived and the second eldest was Napoleon. This portrait of her dates from 1800 to 1804, the period when Napoleon was consul, and shows her seated with a view through to the Tuileries. Her son is represented in the sculpted bust in the background and is depicted as consul. The sculpture is fairly close in type to a consular bust of Napoleon of 1800 by Louis-Simon Boizot. Several other portraits of Madame Mère by Gérard survive. This one had a particularly interesting history. It was given by Napoleon to his younger brother Jerome, King of Westphalia (1807–13), who was later forced, for financial reasons, to marry off his daughter Mathilde to Anatole, one of the spectacularly rich Demidoff family. The portrait evidently went with her for it ended up first in the Musée de San Martino on the island of Elba, and then in the Demidoff family's villa of San Donato, just outside Florence, from where it was sold in 1880.

Oil on canvas,
210.8 × 129.8
Purchased with the aid of
the National Art Collections
Fund 1988
NG 2461

François-Xavier Fabre 1766–1837
Portrait of a Man 1809

Oil on canvas, 61.5 × 50
Purchased with the aid of
the National Art Collections
Fund 1992
NG 2548

Fabre is now perhaps best known for the museum he founded in his native Montpellier, and to which he gave his name, the Musée Fabre. It houses one of the great provincial collections in France. A former pupil of Jacques-Louis David, Fabre spent much of his working life in Italy, at first in Rome (he won the Prix de Rome in 1787) and then from 1793 in Florence. There he formed a close friendship with the poet Vittorio Alfieri and his mistress the Countess of Albany, widow of Charles Edward Stuart. Fabre painted portraits, history paintings and landscapes and was also a passionate collector. This portrait of an unknown young man bears a partially legible pencil inscription on the unpainted edge of the canvas M Camille and is dated 1809. It was probably painted, therefore, in Paris in the last months of 1809 during a visit Fabre paid to France between September 1809 and October 1810. The sitter's elegantly dishevelled hair is cut in the then fashionable antique style 'à la Titus' and is most beautifully depicted by the artist in one of his finest and most sensitive portraits.

François-Xavier Fabre 1766–1837
View of Florence from the North Bank of the Arno 1813

One of the greatest of all neoclassical landscape paintings, this view of Florence is dated 1813 and looks back in style to the classically balanced landscapes of such seventeenth-century masters as Claude Lorrain and Nicolas Poussin. The view, which would have been composed in the studio, probably based on drawings made on the spot, is from the north bank of the Arno looking east. It shows, in the mid-distance, the watermill, la Mulina della Vagaloggia, built in the fourteenth century and demolished in 1854 to make way for the Lungarno Vespucci. The trees in

the foreground were also displaced then. The weir that runs diagonally across the river from it to the south bank survives. Beyond is the Palazzo della Signoria, and to the left the dome of the cathedral, Santa Maria del Fiore. Fabre often included views of Florence in the background of his portraits, most notably in his *Allen Smith Seated Above the Arno* of 1797, now in the Fitzwilliam Museum, Cambridge.

Oil on canvas, 96 × 135
Purchased with the aid of the Galloway Anderson Fund and the National Art Collections Fund 1998
NG 2692

Camille Corot 1796–1875 · Ville-d'Avray: Entrance to the Wood

Corot is often seen as the major linking figure between the neoclassical landscapists of the early nineteenth century and the Impressionists, whose earliest works date from the 1860s. He was taught by the former (his masters were Bertin and Michallon), and he knew and certainly influenced the latter. His early work was very much shaped by his first trip to Italy (1825–8) and displays a remarkable naturalism, especially in the oil-sketches painted directly from nature. From the 1850s onwards, however, Corot developed a greyer, more diaphanous style, which can now seem repetitive and mannered. Nevertheless, it was these later works which proved extremely popular with collectors in France and Britain in the nineteenth century.

This charming little view was made at Ville-d'Avray, the small town to the west of Paris where Corot's parents had a modest country house with grounds. It was probably painted around 1825, just before Corot left for Italy, and was retouched later around 1850. Looking at such a freshly painted composition, it is easy to understand how Constable's landscapes, similar in many respects, enjoyed such popularity when they were exhibited in Paris in the mid-1820s.

Oil on canvas, 46 × 35
Purchased with the aid of
A.E. Anderson in memory of
his brother Frank 1927
NG 1681

Paul Guigou 1834–1871 · *The Olive Trees* 1860

Guigou was one of the leading figures in the school of landscape painting which developed in Provence in the south of France in the middle of the nineteenth century. He moved to Paris in 1862 and knew all the major Impressionists but was not influenced by them; his pictures retained the strong and idiosyncratic colouring typical of the brightly-lit Provençal landscape. His work provides a fascinating example of an alternative tradition to Impressionism (essentially a Paris-based movement) which was, nevertheless, equally concerned with the depiction of light in the landscape. Guigou devoted himself to painting full-time in 1861. This picture dates from one year earlier, when he was still a law student. He exhibited it at the Salon in Montpellier where it attracted favourable comment. The harshness of the Provençal landscape is illustrated by features such as the two goats in the foreground nibbling at the sparse vegetation and the seated goatherd sheltering under one of the olive trees against a backdrop of steep and arid hills.

Oil on canvas,
68.2 × 104.1
Purchased 1988
NG 2462

Gustave Courbet 1819–1877 · The Wave

Oil on canvas, 46 × 55
Presented by Sir Alexander
Maitland in memory of his
wife Rosalind 1960
NG 2233

Courbet was the great rebel of nineteenth-century French art. He was born in the Jura, a mountainous region in the east of France bordering on Switzerland. His uncompromising view of nature must have been partly conditioned by his upbringing amidst the rugged landscape there, and he remained, quite deliberately, an outsider in the Parisian art world which he first entered in the late 1840s. Indeed, at the time of the great Universal Exhibition in Paris in 1855 he set up his own exhibition in his so-called Pavilion of Realism. This was in direct opposition to the officially sanctioned art shown at the exhibition from which his great allegory The Studio (Musée d'Orsay, Paris) had been rejected. Courbet's last years were spent in exile in Switzerland.

Courbet was a highly physical man and he was fascinated by the power of the sea. He spent the summer of 1869, the probable date of this picture, at Etretat on the Normandy coast and painted a number of pictures of waves breaking on the shore. The motif of the single wave was adapted from Japanese colour prints which were widely available on the Paris art market in the 1860s.

Charles-François Daubigny 1817–1878 · *Orchard in Blossom* 1874

Like Corot and Théodore Rousseau, Daubigny was one of the major landscapists of the generation which immediately preceded the Impressionists. Nevertheless, when he became a member of the Salon jury in the 1860s he was greatly supportive of younger artists such as Cézanne, Pissarro and Renoir. As a young man Daubigny had tried and failed twice to win the Prix de Rome for Historical Landscape. Although he did visit Italy in 1836, he concentrated for the rest of his life on the landscape of France, in particular, the scenery around the River Oise north of Paris, where he finally settled in the little town of Auvers in 1859. His naturalistic landscapes, with their often dramatic lighting and weather effects, are frequently cited as direct precursors of Impressionism.

Daubigny painted scenes of orchards from 1857 onwards. They were greatly admired by many of the Impressionists and Post-Impressionists, especially by Van Gogh who also painted a memorable series of orchard scenes. Van Gogh very much associated Daubigny with 'the Norman apple tree'.

Oil on canvas, 85 × 157
Purchased 1993
NG 2586

Camille Pissarro 1830–1903 · *The Marne at Chennevières*

Oil on canvas,
91.5 × 145.5
Purchased 1947
NG 2098

Pissarro was slightly older than many members of the Impressionist movement and his early work shows strong debts to the preceding generation of landscape painters such as Corot and Daubigny. In the later 1860s and 1870s he had been in the mainstream of Impressionism but then, in the mid-1880s, he was very much taken up with the art and theories of Seurat and the Neo-Impressionists. This large riverscape was painted in 1864–5 and was exhibited at the Paris Salon in 1865. The diagonal composition shows the influence of Daubigny, while the extensive use of the palette knife would have been derived from Courbet. At the time he painted this picture Pissarro was renting a house at La Varenne-Saint-Hilaire, a village to the south-east of Paris and situated on the River Marne. Some of the buildings of this village are visible on the left bank, while the church and houses of Chennevières can be seen in the distance at the top of the bank on the right. In the middle distance there is a small boat, possibly a ferry, carrying five people, one of whom carries a parasol. Modern life intrudes into this idealised riverscape in the shape of the small factory buildings on the right bank.

Camille Pissarro 1830–1903 · *Kitchen Gardens at L'Hermitage, Pontoise 1874*

In 1866 Pissarro moved with his family to the hamlet of L'Hermitage, just to the north of Pontoise. Although there were protracted absences, for example, to Louveciennes and then to London during the Franco-Prussian War, Pissarro remained there in a series of rented houses for the majority of the period up to 1883. Situated some twenty-five kilometres north-west of Paris and overlooking the River Oise, Pontoise in Pissarro's day was a market town recently linked by rail to the capital. Its economy was heavily reliant on the agriculture of the Vexin plateau and on the produce of its own market gardens. Just such a garden is depicted in this picture which shows

men and women bringing in the autumn crops, including cabbages and onions. It was painted in 1874, the year of the first Impressionist exhibition and, although it was not included in that show, its technique exhibits many of the hallmarks of Impressionism – broken yet fluid brushwork, bright colouring, and an absence of black or other dark colours in the shadows.

Oil on canvas, 54 × 65.1
Presented by Mrs Isabel M. Traill 1979
NG 2384

Eugène Boudin 1824–1898 · *Trouville Harbour*

Boudin was one of the most important precursors of Impressionism and he also participated in their first group show in 1874. His oil sketches and freshly painted pictures of the Normandy coast were particularly influential on the young Claude Monet, whom he first met in 1858. Boudin's style varied little in the course of a long and prolific career during which his work was promoted by the dealer Durand-Ruel, who also supported the Impressionists.

The port of Trouville, just a few miles to the west of Boudin's native Honfleur, was one of his favourite subjects and he depicted it many times. In this picture of 1873 Boudin shows the view downstream past the line of quays on the right. The long warehouse on the point has been identified as the Hôtel Bellevue.

Oil on panel, 30.7 × 57.6
Bequest of Agnes Anderson; received from the estate of her daughter Mrs Jessie B. Agnew 1979
NG 2371

Alfred Sisley 1839–1899 · Molesey Weir, Hampton Court 1874

Born in Paris of Anglo-French parents, Sisley retained English nationality throughout his life, despite a late attempt in 1898 to become a naturalised Frenchman. He was one of the exhibitors at the first Impressionist exhibition in 1874. His style of painting remained relatively consistent for the rest of his career and witnessed fewer variations and developments than those of his fellow-Impressionists such as Monet, Pissarro or Renoir. Sisley had lived in England (1857–9) and during this period he trained for a career in business before turning to art. He returned briefly in July 1874, to London, possibly in the company of the famous operatic baritone and collector Jean-Baptiste Faure. Faure purchased six of the paintings Sisley executed during this visit, including this one. It shows the view upstream from Hampton Court Bridge, to the

west of London, with Ash Island and the northern bank of the Thames beyond. The weir in the foreground breaks the flow of the Thames to create a floating basin and to direct water into Molesey Lock. Sisley's Impressionist technique splendidly captures the spume and spray of the water as it slides over the weir or crashes through the barrier beyond. The artist was particularly fascinated by scenes involving water and it featured many times in the landscapes he painted back in France in locations such as Marly, Versailles, Saint Mammès and Moret-sur-Loing.

*Oil on canvas, 51.5 × 68.8
Presented by Sir Alexander
Maitland in memory of his
wife Rosalind 1960*
NG 2235

Jules Bastien-Lepage 1848–1884 · Pas Mèche (Nothing Doing) 1882

Oil on canvas,
132.1 × 89.5
Purchased 1913
NG 1133

Bastien-Lepage's earthy, tonal style and his realist subject-matter, concentrating on peasant life, were highly influential on British artists in the later nineteenth century, particularly on the works of the so-called Glasgow Boys such as James Guthrie and E.A. Walton. By contrast, Impressionism, with its much brighter palette, was not really discovered by the British until the early years of the twentieth century.

Pas Mèche was painted for the London dealers Arthur Tooth & Sons and was included in Bastien-Lepage's memorial exhibition in Paris in 1885. The title is an abbreviation of the French slang 'Il n'y a pas mèche', usually taken to mean 'There's nothing doing', an expression which seems to mirror the boy's unconcerned air. He was probably a barge boy and would have used his whip to drive the horses which pulled the vessel and his horn to alert the lockmasters of the barge's impending approach. The rather grim agricultural scenery in the background was possibly based on that near Bastien-Lepage's native Damvillers in the Meuse district of north-eastern France.

Claude Monet 1840–1926 · *A Seascape, Shipping by Moonlight*

Monet is perhaps the most typical of the French Impressionists and his brightly coloured landscapes and cityscapes have become extraordinarily familiar through their frequent reproduction on cards, book covers, and on many other items. The National Gallery of Scotland is fortunate to own five paintings by him. This view of the harbour at Honfleur by moonlight, possibly dating from 1864, is a relatively early work, painted ten years before the first Impressionist exhibition, and is executed in what was for Monet a highly unusual technique of palette knife and brush. The very bold lighting effects thereby achieved contribute to the drama of the scene. Monet later revealed to an American enquirer: 'I greatly admire moonlights and from time to time have made studies from them; but I have never finished any of these studies because I found it so difficult to paint nature at night.' Perhaps his memory was at fault, for this picture, although somewhat cursory in its execution, should probably be classed as finished and was possibly completed in the studio.

Oil on canvas, 60 × 73.8
Purchased 1980
NG 2399

Claude Monet 1840–1926 · *Poplars on the Epte*

Oil on canvas, 81.8 × 81.3
Purchased 1925
NG 1651

Monet undertook his celebrated series of paintings of poplars between the late spring and late autumn of 1891. The trees belonged to the village of Limetz on the River Epte, situated two kilometres from the little town of Giverny where Monet had settled in 1890. The series was painted from a point on the Epte near to where it joins the Seine. Nearly all of the pictures were painted from a boat, in all probability Monet's floating studio. In June 1891 the municipal authorities at Limetz decided to sell the trees at auction as they had reached their ideal height of thirty feet and were ready to be cut down for timber. In partnership with a timber merchant Monet was successful in acquiring the trees at a subsequent sale on 2 August and was able to continue painting them. Fifteen of the series were exhibited by Monet at the Durand-Ruel Gallery in Paris in 1892.

Claude Monet 1840–1926 · *Haystacks: Snow Effect* 1891

Between 1888 and 1891 Monet painted a total of thirty surviving pictures of the stacks of grain which stood in a field just to the west of the house in Giverny that he had rented since 1883 and which he bought in November 1890. The stacks are seen looking to the west or south-west with a low range of hills on the far bank of the Seine about a mile away in the distance. Many of these pictures were painted in a concerted campaign which began in the early autumn of 1890 and continued throughout the following winter, which was relatively mild. Monet persuaded the local farmer to leave the stacks standing throughout this period. Although begun out-of-doors, there can be little doubt that the paintings were completed in the studio. Fifteen pictures from the series were exhibited at the Durand-Ruel Gallery in Paris in 1891, to great critical acclaim. As many later writers have remarked, in paintings such as these Monet achieved a kind of lyrical semi-abstraction which anticipated the concerns of many artists in the twentieth century.

Oil on canvas, 65 × 92
Bequest of Sir Alexander Maitland 1965
NG 2283

Georges Seurat 1859–1891 · A Study for 'Une Baignade'

Oil on panel, 15.9 × 25
Presented by Sir Alexander
Maitland in memory of his
wife Rosalind 1960
NG 2222

The founder of Neo-Impressionism, Seurat was one of the most distinctive and influential artists to emerge in France at the close of the nineteenth century. Born to comfortably-off parents he was able to pursue his artistic interests relatively unfettered by financial worries. He studied at the Ecole des Beaux-Arts in Paris and then undertook military service. In 1880 he began to concentrate on drawing, producing some of the greatest and most atmospheric drawings of the twentieth century in his technique of conté crayon on textured paper. At the same time he was developing a seemingly more rational and scientific manner of painting with which to harness the vibrant colours of Impressionism, viewed by many as a somewhat undisciplined technique. This involved the use of small dots of unmixed colour laid side by side on the canvas producing an 'optical mixture' of extraordinary vibrancy.

Seurat's first major statement using this technique was the large painting *Une Baignade, Asnières* (National Gallery, London). Begun in 1883 and submitted to the 1884 Salon, it was rejected and shown by Seurat instead at the newly formed Groupe des Artistes Indépendants, where a number of critics correctly compared its frieze-like composition both to the art of the Renaissance and to the nineteenth-century painter Puvis de Chavannes. Seurat worked up the composition in a total of ten drawings and thirteen oil sketches (*croquetons*, literally 'sketchettes'), of which this is one. This vivid study, painted on unprimed wood, differs in many respects from the final painting and features a horse being washed in the right foreground. In the distance is the Asnières railway bridge.

Georges Seurat 1859–1891 · Seated Nude: Study for 'Une Baignade'

Preparatory drawings exist for each of the five principal protagonists in Seurat's monumental canvas Une Baignade, Asnières, which depicts a lazy summer's afternoon on the banks of the Seine, in suburban Paris. This study relates to the central bather, who sits quietly by the river's edge, cooling his feet in the water. The drawing appears to have been made as the painting developed, and was apparently used as the final guide for the finished figure, who possesses the same slumped posture, long right arm and thick mop of dishevelled hair.

Evidence of artists' furniture in this and other drawings for the painting, confirms that the studies were made from life models in the confines of Seurat's studio. Here, the boyish nude sits on a box or pedestal draped with cloth. The stillness of his pose is carried over into the painting, in which the youth, languid in the hot sunshine, seems absorbed in deep reverie. The drawing is made on a brand of 'Ingres' paper, favoured by Seurat for its rough texture and milk-white tone (now creamy in colour, after long exposure to light). Particularly suited to chalk-like media, this support enabled Seurat to achieve the grainy, penumbral quality that characterises his tonal drawing style.

Conté crayon on paper,
31.7 × 24.7
Purchased by Private Treaty
1982
D 5110

Georges Seurat 1859–1891 · La Luzerne, Saint-Denis

Oil on canvas, 65.3 × 81.3
Purchased with the aid of
the National Art Collections
Fund, a Treasury Grant and
the family of Roger Fry
1973
NG 2324

This picture may have been begun in 1884 and finished the following year. It depicts the broad plain which in the nineteenth century still separated Paris from Saint-Denis (now a northern suburb of the capital). Across a field of alfalfa (luzerne), punctuated throughout by red poppy flowers, can be seen a low wall and beyond, a row of farm buildings and houses. Space is flattened by the use of a high horizon line. The normal means of creating a sense of spatial recession, such as a winding path or road, have been denied. The viewer is left with a flat yet vibrating composition in which the short and unblended brushstrokes create a complex, flickering pattern. A sensuous use of colour is allied to a certain severity of conception. This painting is one of the most fascinating examples of Seurat's development of what he called 'divisionism', but which his friend the critic Félix Fenéon preferred to call 'pointillism'. Interestingly, it belonged for a while to the English painter and critic Roger Fry (1866–1934) who did so much to introduce British audiences to Impressionism and Post-Impressionism.

Edgar Degas 1834–1917 · A Group of Dancers

This beautiful study of three dancers in front of a mirror in the practice room probably dates from the 1890s. Degas often reworked his designs and there are earlier pastels of the same figure grouping. Direct evidence of Degas's physical involvement can be seen in the fingerprints in the paint surface where he manipulated the paint. In his lifetime Degas was celebrated above all for his depiction of the ballet – over 1,500 paintings, pastels, prints and drawings of dancers by him survive. The ballet provided him with a vast range of poses from which he compiled a highly personal vocabulary of the human body. His own family was deeply interested in the ballet and the opera and this enthusiasm was eagerly taken up by Degas, who numbered among his friends Ludovic Halévy, the famous librettist, and Desiré Dihau, bassoonist at the Paris Opera. It was they who probably provided him with an entrée to the world of corridors, wings and dressing-rooms behind the theatre stage. This sense of a closed world, hidden from public view, would also inform the brothel scenes depicted in Degas's monotype prints.

Oil on paper laid on canvas,
47 × 61.9
Presented by Sir Alexander
Maitland in memory of his
wife Rosalind 1960
NG 2225

Edgar Degas 1834–1917 · *Diego Martelli (1839–1896)*

Oil on canvas,
110.4 × 99.8
Purchased 1932
NG 1785

Born into a comfortably-off family with relatives in Naples and Louisiana, Degas received a classical education and spent time in Italy as a young man. In Paris he became a founder-member of the Impressionist group and organised several of their exhibitions. Highly intelligent and possessed of a sharp wit, he remained somewhat apart from the mainstream, however, and pursued his own interest in essentially figurative art. His later work became increasingly personal in manner as he tirelessly re-examined his favourite themes of the female nude and ballet dancers.

The portrait of Diego Martelli, the Florentine art critic and supporter of the group of Italian artists known as the Macchiaioli, was painted in 1879 and is one of Degas's masterpieces. The apparently random collection of objects on the table was doubtless arranged by the artist to illustrate his belief that such items should be expressive of the sitter's life. Degas was fascinated by unconventional viewpoints and has chosen to depict Martelli, who became a close friend, from above. The object on the back wall is probably the lower part of a multi-coloured circular map of Paris. There is another closely related portrait of Martelli by Degas in Buenos Aires.

Vincent van Gogh 1853–1890 · *Orchard in Blossom (Plum Trees)*

Oil on canvas, 54 × 65.2
Presented by Sir Alexander
Maitland in memory of his
wife Rosalind 1960
NG 2217

With Cézanne and Gauguin, the Dutch painter Van Gogh was the greatest of the artists now known as the Post-Impressionists. His work was distinguished by its increasingly emotional style and content, reflecting his ever more disturbed state of mind, brought about by what medical authorities now suspect may have been a cerebral lesion. The son of a pastor, he trained unsuccessfully for the ministry. He also worked as a picture dealer and, for a short time, as a schoolteacher in England. After spending the years 1881–5 in the Netherlands, he was briefly in Antwerp before arriving in Paris in 1886 where he rapidly assimilated the brighter colouring of the Impressionist technique.

In February 1888 he settled in Arles in the south of France. He moved there for a number of reasons including his health and a desire for the sun and the gayer colours he expected to find in the Midi. This painting may have been intended as an outer wing of a triptych of orchard paintings. Van Gogh probably organised the design with the aid of a rudimentary perspective frame, which he was using at the time to give pictorial depth to the series of fourteen paintings of orchards he made while in Arles. Fifteen months later he was admitted to the asylum at nearby Saint-Rémy.

Vincent van Gogh 1853–1890 · *Olive Trees*

This picture of 1889 is one of fourteen known canvases of olive trees which Van Gogh painted while in the asylum at Saint-Rémy. His correspondence reveals he was fully aware of the association of the olive tree with the Passion story and the episode of Christ in the Garden of Gethsemane on the Mount of Olives. He was also fascinated by the colours generated by the trees: 'The olive trees are very characteristic, and I am struggling to catch them. They are old silver, sometimes with more blue in them, sometimes greenish, bronzed, fading white above a soil which is yellow, pink, violet-tinged or orange, to dull red ochre ... And perhaps one day I shall do a personal impression of them as the sunflowers are for the yellows.' The writhing brushwork so evident in this painting was probably symptomatic of his agitated state of mind at the time. Interestingly, some of the raised paint or impasto of this painting shows the weave of another canvas which must have been pressed onto it, indicating Van Gogh often stored his paintings piled together while the paint was still wet. In May 1890 Van Gogh left Saint-Rémy to be cared for by Dr Gachet at Auvers-sur-Oise to the north of Paris. He shot himself on 27 July and died the following day.

Oil on canvas, 51 × 65.2
Purchased 1934
NG 1803

Paul Gauguin 1848–1903 · *Martinique Landscape* 1887

Oil on canvas, 115 × 88.5
Presented by Sir Alexander
Maitland in memory of his
wife Rosalind 1960
NG 2220

Gauguin, together with Cézanne, was perhaps the most influential of all the artists we now label Post-Impressionist. Whereas Cézanne's achievements were essentially in the realm of form and space, Gauguin concentrated on symbolism and meaning. He came relatively late to art, having begun his professional life as a stockbroker. He was deeply influenced by the first Impressionist exhibition of 1874, participated in their fifth and eighth exhibitions, and devoted himself to painting full-time from 1883 onwards. In addition to his knowledge of Impressionist painting (of which he had become a considerable collector), he was extremely well informed about much Western art of the past. His desire to forge new traditions led him to a profound interest in and experience of non-Western art and culture. In 1887 he travelled with his friend the painter Charles Laval to Panama and then to Martinique in the eastern Caribbean before illness forced him to return to France. In Martinique he painted a series of landscapes, of which this is the finest, which marks his break with orthodox Impressionism. The broken brushwork of Impressionism is replaced by flatter areas of colour, the mysterious and gently glowing hues of which reflect his engagement with an alien terrain. The landscape is also more structured, almost Claudian in its balance, reminding us that Gauguin continually combined both ancient and modern traditions in his art.

Paul Gauguin 1848–1903 · *Three Tahitians* 1899

This dates from Gauguin's second period in Tahiti 1895–1901 (the first had lasted from 1891 to 1893). The two girls shown in this picture recur in several other compositions of this time. Many of his Tahitian works are complex allegories. Here the young man with his back to the viewer appears to be offered a choice between the two women, though what they represent is unclear. It is tempting to suggest a parallel with the classical story of the 'Choice of Hercules' where the hero was forced to choose between vice and virtue. In this South Pacific context, the semi-naked girl would seem to represent goodness of some sort, while the girl with fruit could be a reference to the biblical figure of Eve who tempted Adam with an apple. This suggestive fusion of the primitive and the sophisticated forms a powerful paradox in Gauguin's later work. The final two years of Gauguin's life were spent on the remote island of Hivaoa in the tiny village of Atuona where he died after a large dose of morphine and possibly a heart attack.

Oil on canvas, 73 × 94
Presented by Sir Alexander
Maitland in memory of his
wife Rosalind 1960
NG 2221

Paul Gauguin 1848–1903 · The Vision after the Sermon (Jacob and the Angel) 1888

Oil on canvas, 72.2 × 91
Purchased 1925
NG 1643

Gauguin first moved to Brittany in 1886. It is often said that his interest in the area was inspired by its wild, unspoilt landscape and the ancient traditions, simple faith and distinctive regional dress of its inhabitants. This is certainly true, but it should also be pointed out that Brittany had already been extensively colonised by artists and writers by the late 1870s and many of these cultural tourists were British and American. The pretty little town of Pont-Aven, in the south of Brittany, was particularly popular and it was there that Gauguin painted this picture in 1888, probably between mid-August and mid-September. It has since become one of the most famous images in the history of Western art. The literary source is the passage from Genesis (32: 22–32) which relates how Jacob spent a whole night wrestling with a mysterious angel after fording the Jabbok with his family. It is this episode which has evidently just been described in a sermon by the tonsured curate in the lower right-hand corner of the composition and it has literally come to life in the minds of his Breton congregation. Gauguin described the picture in a letter to Van Gogh: 'for me in this painting the landscape and the fight only exist in the imagination of the people praying after the sermon, which is why there is a contrast between the people, who are natural, and the struggle going on in the landscape which is non-natural and out of proportion'. Gauguin unsuccessfully offered the painting to the church at Pont-Aven and then to the church at nearby Nizon. It was eventually sold at auction in Paris in 1891.

Paul Cézanne 1839–1906 · *Montagne Sainte-Victoire*

Oil on canvas, 55 × 65.4
Presented by Sir Alexander
Maitland in memory of his
wife Rosalind 1960
NG 2236

The son of a banker, Cézanne was brought up in the relative artistic obscurity of Provence, but by 1862 he was settled in Paris and soon entered the circle of the young Impressionists where he struck up a particularly close friendship with Camille Pissarro. Gradually and painstakingly he developed his very individual approach to painting in which he sought to reveal or 'realise' the underlying visual structure of nature as he perceived it. This very deliberate approach distinguished him from the other Impressionists and was particularly influential upon the Cubists who considered him one of the fathers of modern art.

From the mid-1870s onwards Cézanne increasingly retreated from Paris and based himself in his native Aix where his favourite subject was the mountain, Sainte-Victoire, a motif for which he developed a magnificent obsession, tirelessly re-examining it in visual terms. This picture probably dates from the first half of the 1890s and was painted from a position to the south-west of Aix overlooking the valley of the Arc. Its unfinished state points to the close relationship between Cézanne's later oil paintings and his watercolours – the white ground on the canvas acting as the equivalent of the white paper he used for his watercolours.

Paul Cézanne 1839–1906 · *The Big Trees*

During the last decades of his career Cézanne concentrated on two major subject types: open scenes such as his views of the Montagne Sainte-Victoire, and more focused depictions of specific trees, rocks and vegetation. This painting of *c*.1904 clearly belongs to the latter category but is more lyrical and balanced than many of his dramatic paintings of the quarry at Bibémus, for example. Like the Gallery's *Montagne Sainte-Victoire*, this picture has areas of unpainted white canvas, but whether Cézanne regarded it as finished remains unclear. It is a general truism that certain great artists – and one can cite Titian and Constable, to name but two – develop late, lyrical and very personal styles. The same observation can be applied to Cézanne. All inessentials have been dispensed with in this picture and one is left with a composition of deceptive symmetry, the two foreground trees leading the eye through to the solitary slender tree trunk that holds the centre of the composition. There is a related watercolour in a French private collection.

Oil on canvas, 81 × 65
Presented by Mrs Anne
F.Kessler 1958; received
after her death 1983
NG 2206

George Jamesone 1589/90–1644 · Lady Mary Erskine, Countess Marischal 1626

Oil on canvas, 67.3 × 54.6
Purchased 1908
NG 958

An Aberdonian by birth, Jamesone was the first Scottish portrait painter to exercise a lasting influence on the development of portraiture in Scotland. After serving an apprenticeship with a decorative painter in Edinburgh, he established an independent practice in the north-east where his earliest patrons were drawn from burgess and academic society in Aberdeen.

By 1626, when the present portrait was commissioned, Jamesone's clientele encompassed the leading nobility of Scotland. Lady Mary Erskine was the daughter of the 2nd Earl of Mar, a friend of James VI and I and Treasurer of Scotland, and had married the 6th Earl Marischal at the remarkably young age of twelve. The artist, who went on to paint Lady Mary's eldest son, William the 7th Earl Marischal, in 1636, appears to have been on unusually intimate terms with the Erskine family. In 1633 William's younger brother, George, stood godfather to Jamesone's son.

By the late eighteenth century, the *Countess Marischal* had been integrated into a series of likenesses of the children of the 2nd Earl of Mar of which several had been contributed by Jamesone and which may have been conceived as a family portrait gallery. The richness and refinement of surface detail in Lady Mary's portrait is exceptional in Jamesone's surviving work. He is otherwise extensively represented in the collection of the Scottish National Portrait Gallery.

Richard Waitt active from 1708–d.1732 · *Still Life* 1724

One of the most elusive Scottish artists of the early eighteenth century, Waitt made his debut as a heraldic painter and portraitist in Edinburgh where he probably trained in the studio of John Scougal, a prolific member of the Scougal dynasty of portrait painters. From 1713 to 1715 Waitt was intensively patronised by the chieftain of Clan Grant of Castle Grant, Strathspey, for whom he painted an ambitious series of portraits of the laird himself, his family, his champion, and his piper, William Cummine (National Museums of Scotland). Between 1715 and 1722, however, there is an unexplained hiatus in the artist's career. In 1707 he had married into an Episcopalian family of Jacobite persuasion. Circumstantial evidence suggests that Waitt may have emigrated to America after the 1715

Jacobite Rising, returning by 1722 when Grant patronage resumed.

Waitt's occasional experimentation with still life, a rare genre in contemporary Scottish painting, probably dates from this later phase of his career. Completed in 1724, the Gallery's picture is one of only two surviving examples, the other being in a Scottish private collection. Although distantly related to seventeenth-century Dutch prototypes, Waitt's striking compositions were probably painted in Scotland and conceivably as commissions for aristocratic patrons. Most of the vegetables depicted by Waitt are known to have been cultivated in the gardens of the wealthy by the 1680s. Wheaten, as distinct from rye, bread was still a luxury commodity in Scotland in the 1720s.

Oil on canvas, 59 × 77.5
Purchased 1978
NG 2366

James Norie Senior 1684–1757 · *Classical Landscape with Architecture* 1736

Oil on canvas, 68 × 136
Purchased 1931
NG 1768

By the mid 1730s the Norie dynasty of painters, headed by James Norie senior, dominated the production of decorative landscape compositions in the Edinburgh locality and, effectively, in the whole of Scotland. Of Morayshire origin, Norie probably received his formative training from the Edinburgh coach and ornamental painter Thomas Warrender whose allegorical *Still Life* is one of the most enigmatic early Scottish paintings in the Gallery's collection. Norie's independent success was to contribute to the demise of his former master's business in 1720.

James Norie's enterprise was supported by at least two of his sons, his youngest son Robert, and James junior who joined his father in signing the Charter of the Edinburgh Academy of St Luke, the earliest art academy in the Scottish capital, in 1729. Essentially house painters, the Nories were highly accomplished craftsmen with the additional capacity to execute easel paintings or murals as a more sophisticated aspect of interior decoration. Designed for insertion into a wall or over a doorway in an aristocratic residence, this picture typifies the Nories' Italianate ideal landscapes in which individual elements of the composition have been derived from a variety of engraved sources. For the Gallery's *Classical Landscape with Architecture*, the Nories borrowed motifs from a view of the Colosseum by the Roman view painter and architect Giovanni Paolo Panini.

A frequent collaborator with his son and namesake, Norie senior made a vital contribution to the later development of landscape painting in Scotland through occasional commissions from aristocratic patrons for topographical paintings of identifiable Scottish landscapes. One of the most fascinating examples of this alternative type of commission is the panoramic view of Taymouth Castle and Loch Tay ordered by the estate proprietor Lord Glenorchy and now in the Scottish National Portrait Gallery.

John Runciman 1744–1768 · King Lear in the Storm 1767

Oil on panel, 44.8 × 61
Bequest of David Laing
1879
NG 570

Of the oil paintings which survived John Runciman's deliberate destruction of his own work, the majority are small-scale representations of New Testament themes. Four are held by the National Gallery of Scotland. King Lear in the Storm, his most innovatory and exceptional composition, was completed in Edinburgh during the penultimate year of his life immediately prior to his departure for Italy. Apart from his Neapolitan self-portrait of 1767 (on loan to the Scottish National Portrait Gallery), Runciman's Shakespearean masterpiece is still the principal picture by which he is known.

John Runciman and his elder brother Alexander (1736–85) were among the pioneers of Shakespearean illustration in Scotland. Their fascination with Shakespeare – which Alexander later commemorated in his self-portrait with John Brown debating The Tempest, also on loan to the Portrait Gallery – may have been related to contemporary stage productions in Edinburgh. The most important performances of King Lear took place in 1764 and 1765 at the Canongate Theatre, established in 1747 by the entrepreneurial Edinburgh painter and engraver Richard Cooper senior as the first permanent theatre in Scotland.

John Runciman's picture is among the most inventive of all early Romantic eighteenth-century interpretations. Transcending the heath setting of his literary source, Runciman developed Shakespeare's subsidiary image of a sea storm into an all-encompassing pictorial metaphor, corresponding to the disintegration of the king's mind. The introduction of a sinking ship on the horizon, a motif which Runciman may have derived from Rubens's painting of the shipwreck of the Trojan hero Aeneas, also recalls by association the opening scene of The Tempest whose very title is in itself a metaphor for cataclysmic change with attendant possibilities of destruction or renewal.

Allan Ramsay 1713–1784 · Jean-Jacques Rousseau

Oil on canvas: 74.9 × 64.8
Purchased 1890
NG 820

On the advice of the expatriate Jacobite, Commander Marshal Keith, to whom he had first appealed for protection, Rousseau fled to Britain in January 1766 to escape intensive persecution from the Swiss and French authorities on account of the revolutionary views on society, education and religion expressed in his novel *Emile* and in *Du Contrat Social*. The celebrated French-Swiss social philosopher and moralist arrived in London as a guest of the eminent Scottish philosopher and historian David Hume who had solicited a pension for him from George III.

Within two months of his arrival in 1766 Rousseau had sat willingly to his friend and correspondent Allan Ramsay for this portrait, posed in the famous Armenian costume which aroused the curiosity of London society. Ramsay conceived the portrait as a gift to David Hume, a close personal friend and co-founder with the artist and the economist Adam Smith of the Select Society, the distinguished Edinburgh debating society. Later that year Ramsay painted one of the most memorable portraits of Hume (in the Scottish National Portrait Gallery) as a companion picture to hang beside Rousseau in Hume's parlour.

Initially Rousseau was pleased with his portrait which was generally accounted a great success and had even been inspected by the king. By the summer, however, Rousseau's persecution mania had provoked a notorious and much publicised quarrel with his Scottish host who resorted, reluctantly, to printing Rousseau's principal letter of accusation in self-defence.

Allan Ramsay 1713–1784
The Artist's Wife: Margaret Lindsay of Evelick

In 1743 the artist's first wife, Anne Bayne, daughter of the Professor of Municipal Law at Edinburgh University, died in childbirth at the Ramsays' London home. Eight years later, during a return visit to Scotland, Ramsay encountered Margaret Lindsay, the elder daughter of Sir Alexander Lindsay of Evelick and niece of the Lord Chief Justice, 1st Earl of Mansfield. On 1 March 1752 she eloped with Ramsay in Edinburgh, the marriage taking place the same day in the Canongate Kirk without the consent of her parents. The Lindsays, who deplored the social inequality of this alliance, immediately severed all relations. As Ramsay's wife, Margaret Lindsay was constantly snubbed in London society on account of her husband's occupation and despite his recognised eminence. Only on Sir Alexander's death was any reconciliation effected with Lady Lindsay.

This tender study of Margaret Ramsay may well commemorate the birth of their second daughter Charlotte in September 1758. By far the most famous of all Ramsay's portraits, it epitomises the most exquisite qualities of his mature style in female portraiture following his return from his second visit to Italy (1754–7). The picture originally hung in Ramsay's London house in Soho Square.

Oil on canvas, 74.3 × 61.9
Bequest of Lady Murray of
Henderland 1861
NG 430

Allan Ramsay 1713–1784
Head of Margaret Lindsay, the Artist's Second Wife, Looking Down

Thought originally to date to the Ramsays' Italian sojourn of 1754–7, this drawing is now bracketed with a group of chalk studies that were made by Ramsay on the island of Ischia in 1776, during his third visit to Italy.

A serious injury to his right arm led to Ramsay's increasing devotion in old age to literary pursuits. During his final two trips to Italy, in 1775–7 and 1782–4, he concentrated on a scholarly treatise (unpublished) exploring the site of Horace's Sabine villa. Margaret accompanied him on his research, assuming the role of his assistant and scribe. This tender and intimate drawing is an outstanding example of Ramsay's lifelong quest for a more natural and informal style of portraiture. Margaret is portrayed with her head tilted forward, eyes cast downwards and lips slightly parted, as if reading aloud, or receiving dictation (a pose which would have been particularly familiar and personal to her husband). The work's feathery execution is typical of Ramsay's later draughtsmanship and reflects the influence of contemporary French artists, such as Maurice-Quentin de La Tour and Jean-Marc Nattier.

This study belongs to a large body of drawings by Ramsay, which passed by descent to the artist's nephew, the Scottish judge Lord Murray of Henderland, in memory of whom they were gifted to the Gallery in 1860. The collection includes many preparatory studies for finished portraits, and represents the principal holding of Ramsay's graphic oeuvre worldwide.

Red chalk with white heightening on grey paper,
37 × 27.9
Lady Murray of Henderland Gift 1860, in
memory of her husband, Lord Murray of
Henderland
D 2009

Robert Adam 1728–1792 · Cullen Castle, Banffshire

Pen and brown ink and grey
wash, over black chalk on
paper, 35.6 × 51
Purchased 1991
D 5325

Robert Adam, in partnership with his brothers, ran one of the most successful and fashionable architectural firms in eighteenth-century Britain. Raised and educated in Edinburgh, he began his career in the practice of his father, William Adam, Scotland's leading architect during the second quarter of the eighteenth century. Robert developed a distinctive and innovative neoclassical style, greatly influenced by his early study in Italy. Kedleston Hall in Derbyshire, Syon House in Middlesex and Culzean Castle in Ayrshire number among his finest achievements.

Throughout his career Robert made hundreds of picturesque drawings, exploring the relationship between buildings and their settings. It has been argued that these works played an important role in the evolution of his architectural designs, helping him to establish mood and composition. The Adam family enjoyed a long professional association with Cullen Castle, then the northern seat of the Earls of Findlater and Seafield. Situated in Banffshire in north-east Scotland, the castle is idyllically located overlooking a dramatic woodland bowl and encircled by extensive landscaped gardens. Prominent in this watercolour is the large single-span bridge, built by William Adam in 1744. Although this work probably presents a reasonably accurate record of Cullen as it was during the 1770s and 1780s, the scene is nonetheless romanticised. Adam adopts a low viewpoint and attenuates proportions to accentuate the castle's grand surroundings.

Jacob More 1740–1793 · *The Falls of Clyde (Cora Linn)*

Oil on canvas,
79.4 × 100.4
Bequest of James Ramsay
MacDonald 1938
NG 1897

In 1767 Jacob More's stage scenery for the New Theatre in Edinburgh was so favourably received that he determined to specialise in landscape painting exclusively. That year his former master Alexander Runciman, who had trained in the Norie tradition of decorative painting, left for Italy, thus affording More an opportunity to dominate the practice of landscape painting in the Scottish capital. The exhibition of the first set of his views of the Falls of Clyde at the Incorporated Society of Artists in London in 1771 transformed More into one of Britain's leading landscape painters who also enjoyed celebrity status in his native Edinburgh.

In 1773, when Dr Johnson undertook his famous tour of the Hebrides in the company of James Boswell, his desire to visit Scotland was still considered eccentric. By the close of the century Scotland was well established as a tourist destination, a process in which the publication of illustrated travel literature was complemented by landscape painting. More's celebration of the 'sublime and terrible' prospects of the three great falls on the Clyde confirmed their central place in an artistic tradition in which later Scottish artists including Alexander Nasmyth followed More's example. The Gallery's picture, which was purchased by Sir Joshua Reynolds from the 1771 London exhibition, was subsequently owned by the Scottish portrait painter David Martin and the Edinburgh landscape painter and drawing master, George Walker.

From the winter of 1771/2 More settled permanently in Italy where, as a prominent member of the expatriate Scots community, he became known internationally as 'More of Rome' and the outstanding British neoclassical landscape painter of his time. Apart from his compatriot Gavin Hamilton, More was the only eighteenth-century Scottish painter to achieve a lasting contemporary reputation abroad.

Gavin Hamilton 1723–1798
Achilles Lamenting the Death of Patroclus

Oil on canvas,
227.3 × 391.2
Purchased 1976
NG 2339

In 1744 Hamilton left for Italy to train with Agostino Masucci, President of the Accademia di San Luca, the art academy in Rome. From 1756, after a brief interlude in London dedicated through financial necessity to portraiture, Hamilton settled permanently in Rome, a milieu which offered greater scope and the promise of international patronage for his preferred vocation in 'great and heroick' history painting. His classical education at Glasgow University predisposed him towards the most influential project of his entire career, the interpretation of Homer's *Iliad* whose rich and extended narrative lent itself naturally to a pictorial cycle.

The first to be executed in Hamilton's set of six illustrations of the *Iliad*, based on Alexander Pope's freely paraphrased verse translations of the original Greek, was *Andromache Bewailing the Death of Hector*. A highly wrought compositional study for the finished picture, which was shipped to London for exhibition in 1762, is in the Gallery's collection. Hamilton's model for the figure of Helen of Troy was an existing patron, the famous beauty Elizabeth Gunning, Duchess of Hamilton. The second picture in order of completion and, arguably, the finest in the series, was *Achilles Lamenting the Death of Patroclus*, painted in Rome between 1760 and 1763 for Sir James Grant prior to being launched by the Society of Artists in London in 1765. Through Cunego's engravings Hamilton's Homeric illustrations achieved international circulation, earning him recognition as a pioneering exponent of European Neoclassicism and the admiration of leading artists in his generation and in the following from Jacques-Louis David to Tobias Sergel and Benjamin West.

David Allan 1744–1796 · The Connoisseurs: John Caw (died 1784), John Bonar (1747–1807) and James Bruce · 1783

In 1780, following an abortive attempt to establish his career in London, David Allan settled in Edinburgh, lodging initially at Hopetoun House with the Hope family whose sponsorship had enabled him to travel to Italy in 1767. Among Allan's other influential patrons and mentors was the 11th Earl of Buchan to whom the artist confided, in 1780, his frustration concerning the lack of patronage for history painting in Britain and, by extension, the necessity of earning a living through portraiture in a 'small, domestic and conversational style'. The formula of the conversation piece, a type of portraiture first practised in Scotland by Gawen Hamilton (c.1697–1737), was successfully extended by Allan to incorporate topographical 'portraits' of the patron's residence, as in The Halkett of Pitfirrane Family of 1781 in the Gallery's collection.

Allan's return to Scotland coincided with the founding of the Society of Antiquaries of Scotland in Edinburgh by the 11th Earl of Buchan. Buchan may well have acted as the intermediary in securing a commission three years later to paint this conversation piece of Edinburgh connoisseurs of whom the oldest, the excise officer John Caw (seated on the left), had deposited his private collection of coins, medals and fossils with the society in 1782. In 1783, the year of the commission, Allan presented to the Antiquaries a gold medal awarded to him for history painting by the Academy of St Luke in Rome. In so doing, he may have been soliciting the Antiquaries' assistance to obtain patronage. Caw is shown examining an engraving after Raphael's celebrated painting St John the Baptist in the Wilderness in the Tribuna of the Uffizi in Florence, an advertisement for the cultural sophistication of Allan's patrons and a reminder of the artist's own aspirations towards history painting which had been fostered by a ten year residence in Italy.

Oil on canvas,
87.5 × 101.9
Purchased 1963
NG 2260

Sir Henry Raeburn 1756–1823
Revd Dr Robert Walker (1755–1808) Skating on Duddingston Loch

This lovely portrait, in character quite unlike any other known paintings by Raeburn, has been the focus of more speculation concerning its date, the authorship and the identity of the sitter than any other single painting in the Gallery's Scottish collection. The sitter is thought to be the Reverend Robert Walker, minister of the Canongate Kirk, who had joined the Edinburgh Skating Society in 1780. This prestigious club, the oldest established in Britain, was noted for its commitment to figure skating, described by Lord Cockburn as 'the poetry of motion', and usually convened at Lochend or Duddingston. The exquisitely elegant pose adopted by the Reverend Walker was the result of diligent practice of the 'travelling position' and required considerable sophistication.

The essential idea for the picture whether of the artist's or the sitter's conception, may have originated in Gilbert Stuart's monumental skating portrait of the London-based Scottish lawyer William Grant of Congleton (National Gallery of Art, Washington DC). By the mid 1790s, when Raeburn was probably painting Walker, Grant's portrait had been shipped from London to Edinburgh. The entrancing qualities of Raeburn's skater, which has become an international icon for the National Galleries of Scotland, were recognised within his lifetime. In 1813, during one of his winter visits to his native Edinburgh, the expatriate Scottish portrait painter Andrew Geddes paid a direct tribute to Raeburn in a commissioned portrait of the Edinburgh Skating Society's young secretary, Charles Knowles Robison.

Oil on canvas, 76.2 × 63.5
Purchased 1949
NG 2112

Sir Henry Raeburn 1756–1823
Colonel Alastair Ranaldson Macdonell of Glengarry (1771–1828)

Sir Walter Scott's pen portrait of Macdonell of Glengarry captured to perfection the anachronistic and idiosyncratic lifestyle of his close friend and contemporary on whom he probably based the character of the doomed Jacobite clan chieftain Fergus McIvor in his novel *Waverley*: 'This gentleman is a kind of Quixote in our age, having retaind in its full extent whole feelings of Clanship and Chieftainship elsewhere so long abandoned. He seems to have lived a century too late and to exist in a state of complete law and order like a Glengarry of old whose will was law to his sept.' Yet, despite his passion for the customs and social structures of Gaelic culture of the era prior to the Forty-Five Jacobite Rising, Glengarry evicted his tenants to clear the land for sheep farming. His life ended with appropriate high drama when he leapt from the canal steamer *Stirling Castle* as it grounded in Loch Linnhe. He suffered mortal injuries and his passing was mourned by Scott at the Celtic Society's dinner in January 1828.

The precise circumstances in which Glengarry sat to Raeburn remain unknown although the portrait was presumably completed shortly before its exhibition at the Royal Academy in London in 1812. The proscription on the wearing of Highland dress which followed the Forty-Five Rising had been lifted in 1782. Glengarry may well have wished to emulate, in changed times and with romantic panache, the flamboyant public image of Highland chieftainship which Raeburn had so memorably purveyed in his great full-length portrait of Sir John Sinclair of Ulbster in the late 1790s.

Oil on canvas,
241.9 × 151.1
Purchased 1917
NG 420

Alexander Nasmyth 1758–1840
Princes Street with the Commencement of the Building of the Royal Institution 1825

Oil on canvas,
122.5 × 165.5
Presented by Sir David
Baird 1991
NG 2542

This spectacular city view is a particularly fine example of the mature work of Nasmyth whom Wilkie honoured as the 'founder of the landscape painting school of Scotland'. A pupil of Alexander Runciman, who himself had trained with the Nories, Nasmyth was employed by Allan Ramsay as a specialist drapery painter in his London studio before establishing his own successful portrait practice in Edinburgh. During the 1790s Nasmyth evolved his most influential type of landscape painting – large-scale panoramic views in which topographical accuracy was united with a distinctive picturesque sensibility. Nasmyth's manner was widely disseminated through his classes for amateurs and intending professional artists which convened at his custom-built premises at 47 York Place in Edinburgh.

Nasmyth's panorama records both the city itself and its burgeoning cultural life at a dramatic stage of transition. From a vantage point at the junction of Hanover Street and Princes Street, the artist's outlook encompasses both the late mediaeval Old Town and the neoclassical New Town with a vista towards Arthur's Seat and the Nelson Monument on Calton Hill. On the right, emerging from a building site on the artificial earthen mound, is the Royal Institution building commissioned from William Henry Playfair, one of the principal architects of the New Town, as a Doric temple to the arts. Opened in 1826, the new building served as the venue for the Institution's pioneering exhibitions of Old Master and contemporary Scottish painting and included accommodation for the art school known as the Trustees' Academy and ultimately for the Royal Scottish Academy formed in 1826. Playfair later designed the adjacent National Gallery of Scotland, of which the foundation stone was laid in 1850.

John Knox 1778–1845
Landscape with Tourists at Loch Katrine

Oil on canvas, 90 × 125
Purchased 1992
NG 2557

An obscure and yet surprisingly influential figure in the evolution of early nineteenth-century Scottish landscape painting, Knox was raised in Paisley and migrated to Glasgow where, by 1809, he was specialising in portraiture. By the following decade, when he published a series of lithographs after his own Scottish views, he was in demand as a landscape painter, noted for the sweeping breadth of his effects and precise rendering of specific topographical detail. These qualities found their most impressive expression in a pair of panoramic views from Ben Lomond of which one set was acquired by the Duke of Hamilton and is on loan to the National Gallery of Scotland. Through his drawing-classes in Glasgow, attended by Horatio McCulloch, William Leighton Leitch and Daniel Macnee, Knox's pictorial ideas were transmitted to his successors in Scottish landscape and portrait painting.

Knox was among the first generation of Scottish artists to be captivated by Sir Walter Scott's poem *The Lady of the Lake*, published in 1810. Scott portrayed Loch Katrine as an inviolate sanctuary of peaceful beauty where the exiled Douglas and his daughter Ellen discover an idyllic retreat from their former existence at court. The enchantment worked by Scott's painterly evocation of the Trossachs extended beyond the immediate setting of the poem itself to encompass much of the rest of the Highlands, opening up 'the land of the mountain and the flood' to mass tourism. In this striking composition Knox reinterpreted with dramatic intensity the classical tradition of landscape painting inherited from Alexander Nasmyth and ultimately derived from the work of Claude Lorrain. In the left foreground two expectant visitors, attended by a piper, are shown waiting to board the ferry to Ellen's Isle.

Sir David Wilkie 1785–1841 · *Pitlessie Fair* 1804

Oil on canvas,
61.5 × 110.5
Purchased 1921
NG 1527

In 1799 the precociously gifted fourteen-year-old Wilkie, son of the parish minister of Cults in Fife, entered the Trustees' Academy in Edinburgh where his fellow students included William Allan and John Burnet, subsequently Wilkie's memorialist and principal engraver. By 1802 the drawing academy's elementary curriculum had been restructured to incorporate oil painting and a system of annual premiums for the best historical composition. Two years later Wilkie began his first major subject picture, a complex vernacular narrative 'portrait' of the annual May fair which took place in Pitlessie village in the vicinity of his native Cults. This radical, and ultimately extremely influential, departure from the prescribed conventions of history painting in the grand manner was to establish the fundamental orientation of Wilkie's later career.

As an alternative source of inspiration, Wilkie was able to draw upon the growing literary cult of the indigenous, folkloric and traditional aspects of Scottish life and the equivalent in painting in the work of David Allan and Alexander Carse whose watercolour of *Oldhamstocks Fair* (1796) is in the Gallery's collection. Wilkie's own scheme of composition also displays a marked affinity with the village scenes by seventeenth-century Flemish and Dutch genre painters such as Teniers and Van Ostade which he probably knew from engravings. Conspicuously experimental and lacking in integration, Wilkie's human panorama represents a complete cross-section of Fifeshire rural society, many of the individual fairgoers being actual parishioners whom the artist had secretly sketched in church. In 1805, with the permission of Charles Kinnear of Kinloch, the local landowner who had commissioned *Pitlessie Fair*, Wilkie took the finished picture to London as his showpiece and prospectus.

Sir David Wilkie 1785–1841 · The Letter of Introduction 1813

In 1805 Wilkie made his decisive move to London and the Royal Academy Schools with their superior facilities for art education. He carried with him *Pitlessie Fair* which was seen by Samuel Whitbread and by the Earl of Mansfield, both of whom awarded him commissions. The following year the exhibition of *The Village Politicians*, painted for Lord Mansfield and now displayed at Scone Palace, Perthshire, drew prodigious crowds at the Royal Academy and prompted a commission for *The Blind Fiddler* (Tate Gallery, London) from Sir George Beaumont. In 1809, at the exceptionally young age of twenty-four and having exhibited only five paintings, Wilkie was elected an Associate of the Royal Academy.

Wilkie's meteoric rise to metropolitan fame belied the actual circumstances of his arrival in London. Until the Royal Academy exhibition of 1806 he had barely subsisted on portraiture and had actually contemplated returning to Scotland. In *The Letter of Introduction*, he recreated, in fictitious form, a specific recollection of adversity when he was snubbed by the connoisseur Caleb Whitefoord on presenting a letter of introduction from Sir George Sandilands in 1805. It is debatable whether Wilkie ever surpassed the understated yet astringent wit of *The Letter of Introduction* in which the tense interaction of the two incompatible personalities is dependent on the slightest indications of posture, facial expression, and hands, supported by all the accessories of the interior. The pictorial legacy of this single picture was perpetuated throughout the nineteenth century by lesser artists who adapted Wilkie's basic compositional formula for a variety of emotionally charged encounters.

Oil on panel, 61 × 50.2
Purchased 1938
NG 1890

Sir David Wilkie 1785–1841 · Distraining for Rent 1815

Oil on panel, 81.3 × 123
Purchased 1975
NG 2337

Wilkie embarked on *Distraining for Rent*, essentially his unique venture in tragic genre, on his return from a visit to Paris in July 1814. The unrelieved solemnity of the picture and the evident strength of its moral conviction disconcerted many admirers of the artist and challenged existing preconceptions about his commitment to sophisticated comedy of manners.

Wilkie's biographer Allan Cunningham and his engraver Abraham Raimbach both traced the genesis of the picture to Wilkie's personal experience during his one-man exhibition of 1812 when bailiffs seized pictures from the hired premises in settlement of the debts of a previous tenant. The context of the picture was, however, entirely rural, focusing on the imminent eviction of the defaulting tenant farmer (the pivotal figure on the left of the table, slumped in despair). The prospect of a lasting peace on the conclusion of the Napoleonic wars engendered widespread apprehension of financial collapse for farmers contending with the competitive prices of imported corn. These fears were exacerbated by bitter wrangling in parliament over the Corn Laws in 1814 and 1815, coinciding exactly with the composition of Wilkie's picture.

The topicality of rural dispossession induced some of Wilkie's wealthier patrons to interpret *Distraining for Rent* as an emotive attack on the land-owning classes. Yet in 1815, when the painting was shown at the British Institution in London, it was purchased by the equally patrician directors as part of their new policy of promoting living artists and building a national collection of British art. They clearly recognised the calibre of Wilkie's first attempt to deploy his skills in psychological interplay in the expression of deep and tragic emotions.

Sir David Wilkie 1785–1841 · The Greenwich Pensioner 1823

Wilkie numbers among Britain's greatest draughtsmen. The majority of his drawings, from scrappy pen and ink scribbles, to elaborately finished watercolours, relate to the complex and protracted evolution of his paintings. Most of these studies had a purely functional purpose and were never intended for display.

Shown in the Royal Academy's annual exhibition of 1824, this sheet was one of the very few drawings that Wilkie deemed fit to exhibit. Cunningham, Wilkie's biographer, relates how during the long and troublesome development of the painting *The Entrance of George IV at Holyroodhouse, Edinburgh* (Royal Collection), the artist found solace in sketching favourite subjects. This work was drawn during a chance visit to the Royal Hospital at Chelsea, London, and depicts one of the resident 'pensioners', attired in the institution's distinctive uniform. Founded by Charles II in 1682, the hospital was established as a place of refuge and shelter for British military veterans who, through long service or battle wounds, had been reduced to poverty. Wilkie was fascinated by this retired naval serviceman, whose crusty looks seemed to him to epitomise the temperamental Commodore Trunnion, a colourful character from *The Adventures of Peregrine Pickle* (1751) by the Scots-born novelist Tobias Smollet. The pensioner's hooded eyes, which avert the artist's stare, are startlingly keen, suggesting the aged mariner's acuity of mind. Arguably one of Wilkie's finest drawings, the work was reproduced in aquatint by F.C. Lewis in 1826.

Pencil, black chalk and watercolour on paper,
36.4 × 25.1
Purchased 1929
D 3732

Sir William Allan 1782–1820 · The Murder of David Rizzio

Oil on panel,
102.5 × 163.3
Presented by the 3rd Baron
Strathcona and Mount
Royal 1927
NG1677

David Wilkie and William Allan, an apprentice coach-painter, emerged from the first generation of Scottish painters who benefited from the radical reform of the Trustees' Academy, the school of industrial and applied design founded in Edinburgh in 1760. In 1802 the elementary curriculum was extended through the introduction of oil painting, complemented by a system of annual premiums for the best historical composition in accordance with the practice of the Royal Academy Schools in London. Under the influence of Sir Walter Scott, his great admirer and champion, Allan pioneered, with Wilkie, the painting of major pictures illustrative of Scottish history. As Master of the Trustees' Academy himself from 1826, Allan exercised a decisive influence on the following generation including George Harvey and James Drummond.

By the turn of the eighteenth century the cult of Mary, Queen of Scots in British history painting had become self-perpetuating. Within Allan's lifetime, the appearance of Scott's novel The Abbot in 1820 guaranteed her apotheosis as a heroine of romantic fiction. For The Murder of David Rizzio launched at the Royal Academy in London in 1833, Allan consulted The History of Scotland published by William Robertson, the Principal of Edinburgh University, in 1759 and including a supposedly authoritative account of the assassination of Mary's Italian secretary at Holyrood in 1566. The idea for the picture may have germinated during a visit to the Palace of Holyroodhouse with Wilkie in 1817. The deep brown shadows in Allan's composition reflect directly the influence of Wilkie whose picture of John Knox preaching had been exhibited in 1832.

Sir George Harvey 1806–1876 · The Curlers 1835

A pupil of Sir William Allan at the Trustees' Academy, Harvey became a founder-member of the Royal Scottish Academy in 1826 and served as its president throughout the last decade of his life. Like many of Allan's most gifted students, Harvey made a distinctive contribution towards the development of Scottish history painting, specialising in highly charged illustrations of the covenanting struggles of the seventeenth century and of contemporary religious-political turmoil arising from the Disruption of the Church of Scotland in 1843. The popularity of his most emotive Disruption picture, *Quitting the Manse* (in the Gallery's collection) was eclipsed only by that of *The Curlers*.

Conceived as a speculative venture, *The Curlers* was purchased from the Royal Scottish Academy exhibition in 1835 by Sir Gilbert Stirling of Larbert House. Such was the ongoing demand for the picture that Harvey painted a number of copies with minor variations, probably to commission for specific clients. In 1838 William Howison engraved the picture for publication and distribution by one of the most influential publicists of contemporary Scottish painting, the dealer Alexander Hill of Princes Street, Edinburgh, official print seller to the Academy and brother of its Secretary D.O. Hill. The independent success of the engraving earned Howison associate membership of the Academy and transformed Harvey's design into an icon of the sport of curling in Scotland. A detail in vignette was adopted as a frontispiece for the annuals of the Royal Caledonian Curling Club while other details graced the medals struck for a number of regional clubs. The extraordinary appeal of the original was enhanced by its social comprehensiveness. Like Wilkie's *Pitlessie Fair*, *The Curlers* embraced in its composition the whole spectrum of contemporary rural society.

Oil on panel, 55.8 × 167.7
Purchased 1995
NG 2641

William Dyce 1806–1864
Francesca da Rimini 1837

Oil on canvas, 142 × 176
Purchased by the Royal
Scottish Academy 1864;
transferred to the National
Gallery and presented 1910
NG 460

An Aberdonian by birth, Dyce was one of the most artistically gifted and intellectually able of the many Scottish painters who migrated to London in search of greater scope and international prestige. His phenomenally wide range of interests, encompassing medicine, musicology, geology, ecclesiology and art education, has tended to obscure his stature as an easel painter and as the most competent British practitioner of fresco painting in the mid-nineteenth century. By vocation a religious and subject painter, he earned his living in the 1830s as a successful portrait painter in Edinburgh. In 1837, while teaching at the Trustees' Academy, he published his letter to Lord Meadowbank on the reform of Scottish art education and was promptly appointed Superintendent of the new Government School of Design at Somerset House in London.

Dyce regarded *Francesca da Rimini*, an illustration to Dante's epic poem *The Inferno*, as the outstanding achievement of his years in Edinburgh. Francesca, married to an elderly and deformed husband, Giancotto, falls in love with his younger brother Paolo while reading to him. In its original format Dyce's composition included, on the far left, the figure of Giancotto creeping in to murder the lovers by stealth. In 1882 the left edge of the canvas was trimmed, leaving nothing of the malevolent figure other than a disembodied hand which thus became, quite fortuitously, a powerfully suggestive dramatic device. The present frame may have been designed by Sir Joseph Noel Paton who had proposed the reduction of the damaged canvas.

William Dyce 1806–1864
Piety: The Knights of the Round Table about to Depart in Quest of the Holy Grail

When in 1841 the Government appointed a select committee to advise on the decoration of the new Houses of Parliament at Westminster, Dyce was summoned to give evidence on the problems of fresco painting – the medium selected, by virtue of its noble 'High' art associations, for this important state project. Dyce's familiarity with fresco was largely unmatched by his British contemporaries. His expertise owed much to his intimacy with the Nazarenes, a group of modern German painters, greatly influenced by early Renaissance art, who had collaborated on various monumental frescoes in Rome and Munich.

Dyce's interest in German art endeared him to Prince Albert, the active President of the Royal Commission that was constituted to steer the lengthy decoration programme. Following the success of his fresco The Baptism of King Ethelbert for the House of Lords, Dyce was persuaded by the prince to decorate Queen Victoria's Robing Room. The seven principal panels of this scheme were to depict allegories of Christian virtues, as exemplified by the exploits of King Arthur and his knights, related by Sir Thomas Malory in Le Morte d'Arthur. Intended for the largest compartment in the Robing Room, this elaborate symbolisation of 'Piety' was rejected by the Commission when submitted in 1849. Its allusion to the adulterous relationship between Guinevere and Lancelot, who kneels to kiss the queen's hand in sad farewell, was considered improper. According to Malory, the knights' departure presaged the beginnings of the break-up of the Round Table. Dyce's portrayal of Arthur, grieved by the knowledge that many of his men would not return from their quest, and by the consequent threat to his ideal government, was thought too pessimistic an image to associate with Britain's grand new Houses of Parliament.

Watercolour and bodycolour over pencil on buff paper, laid down, 23.3 × 44
Mr Charles Guthrie Gift 1958
D 4788

David Roberts 1796–1864
Rome: Sunset from the Convent of Sant'Onofrio on the Janiculum 1856

Oil on canvas, 213 × 427
Presented by the artist to the
Royal Scottish Academy
1857; transferred to the
National Gallery and
presented 1910
NG 304

In 1851 David Roberts's international renown as a landscape painter was acknowledged by his appointment as a Commissioner for the Great Exhibition under the patronage of the Prince Consort. This celebrity status which he enjoyed during the 1850s has been perpetuated into this century by the prolonged commercial exploitation of his *Views in the Holy Land*, first published during the 1840s. Contemporary impressions of the wonderfully atmospheric colour illustrations to his *Views in the Holy Land*, lithographed from Roberts's original watercolours, are prized as collectors items while modern copies are still widely distributed as definitive souvenirs of pilgrimages and tours to Israel.

In September 1853 Roberts left London for Rome, his chief aim being to paint the interior of St Peter's. While in Rome he made numerous sketches of the city from the particularly fine viewpoint provided by the terrace of the convent of Sant'Onofrio on Mount Janiculum. On his return he exhibited at the Royal Academy in 1855 a panoramic oil painting based on these pencil and watercolour sketches. While Prince Albert hailed it as 'the most magnificent work of art of modern times', the artist and critic John Ruskin was so severely critical that Roberts spent the spring of 1856 re-adjusting the tonal balance of his rose-red sunset. In 1857 the picture was relaunched at the Royal Scottish Academy to whom Roberts presented his partially repainted chef d'oeuvre for eventual inclusion in the permanent collection of the National Gallery of Scotland. Roberts's self-promotional generosity towards the Academy was undoubtedly intended as a tribute to his native Edinburgh and an expression of his abiding attachment to Scotland despite his voluntary exile in London since 1822. A year after the presentation of the picture, Roberts was awarded the freedom of the City of Edinburgh.

Horatio McCulloch 1805–1867
Inverlochy Castle 1857

By the late 1850s McCulloch occupied an extraordinary and almost messianic position in relation to Scottish landscape painting. McCulloch's capacity to distil the romantic essence of the Scottish landscape earned him both critical and popular acclaim as the northern counterpart of Constable and a truly representative 'national' painter, a status which depended on the unquestioning identification of Scotland with the Highlands.

McCulloch's grand Highland views were invariably composed in the studio from carefully prepared sketches executed on the spot in accordance with the common practice of all of his contemporaries. In 1856, during one of his regular summer sketching tours of the West Highlands, McCulloch made a watercolour study of Inverlochy Castle near Fort William. As originally displayed at the Royal Scottish Academy in 1857, the finished picture included in the foreground a group of Highland cattle as picturesque localised detail. The substitution of an empty rowing boat as a device to strengthen the perspective of the composition may have

been intended to intensify the general impression of isolation and desolation, relieved only by the presence of the crofters' cottages in the lee of the castle ruins.

From the 1840s McCulloch had benefited substantially from the steady support of the Edinburgh and Glasgow Art Unions. The Edinburgh association, founded in 1834 as the Royal Association for the Promotion of the Fine Arts in Scotland, was dedicated to the education of public taste and the patronage of contemporary Scottish painting through the outright purchase of original oils and the publication of related reproductive engravings. In 1857 RAPFAS purchased *Inverlochy Castle* from the Academy's exhibition as part of a definitive collection of Scottish art which was ultimately deposited in the National Gallery of Scotland. The engraving commissioned by RAPFAS in 1877 was designed as an illustration to *A Legend of Montrose* by Sir Walter Scott, thus emphasising the indebtedness of McCulloch's particular vision of the Highlands to the Wizard of the North.

Oil on canvas,
91.6 × 152.8
Purchased by RAPFAS
1857; transferred to the
National Gallery 1897
NG 288

James Drummond 1816–1877 · The Porteous Mob 1855

Oil on canvas,
111.8 × 152.5
Purchased by RAPFAS
1856; transferred to the
National Gallery 1897
NG 180

'The profusion of original characters, the Scotch language, Scotch scenery, Scotch men and women ... and the graphic force of the descriptions all struck us with an electric shock of delight.' In recalling the sensational impact of the Waverley novels, the judge, Lord Cockburn, captured the quintessentially pictorial appeal of the *Heart of Midlothian*, the immediate source for Drummond's most theatrical history picture. Scott recounts through a sequence of interrelated narratives the events culminating in the lynching of Porteous, Captain of the Edinburgh City Guard, in the Grassmarket in 1736. In Drummond's picture the serial narrative is telescoped into a single climactic moment. Porteous himself, a tiny figure spreadeagled on the shoulders of his executioners in the middle distance, plays a secondary role to the proliferat-ing sub-plots in the foreground. Scott's vignette of the aristocratic lady assisted from her sedan chair with incongruous civility by one of the lynch mob, has become a complete sub-plot, occupying centre stage. Drummond's unfolding panorama of Scottish life and character, with its reminiscences of Hogarth and Walter Geikie, is dominated by the 'stage-set', reconstructed with the conviction of a committed antiquarian.

In purchasing *The Porteous Mob* in 1856, the Royal Association for the Promotion of the Fine Arts in Scotland acknowledged the centrality of Scottish history painting in the spectrum of contemporary Scottish art. The early curators of the National Gallery were invariably Royal Scottish Academicians. It was no coincidence that the first two, William Borthwick Johnstone and James Drummond, were both promi-nent Scottish history painters.

Thomas Faed 1826–1900 · *Home and the Homeless* 1856

Oil on canvas, 66.7 × 95.6
Purchased 1992
NG 2549

Collectively, the three brothers Faed, Thomas, John (1819–1902) and James (1821–1911) formed the most remarkable dynasty of artists in nineteenth-century Scottish painting. Born near Kirkcudbright, all three migrated to Edinburgh in succession. The training which Thomas and John received from Sir William Allan and Allan's own former pupil, Thomas Duncan, at the Trustees' Academy predisposed both of the Faeds towards domestic genre and the illustration of Scottish history. As a genre painter, Thomas was to enjoy greater commercial success internationally than almost any of his compatriots who moved south to London.

In 1851, encouraged by his acclaimed debut at the Royal Academy, Thomas settled permanently in London. Four years later, *The Mitherless Bairn* (National Gallery of Victoria, Melbourne) was hailed as the Academy's picture of the season. Faed's triumph secured a commission to paint a pendant picture for Baroness Angela Burdett-Coutts, the wealthiest heiress in Britain and a lavish patron of the arts who was later to commission for the city of Edinburgh the bronze statuette of *Greyfriar's Bobby*, sculpted by William Brodie. The philanthropic baroness, popularly known as 'The Queen of the Poor', may well have proposed the theme of *Home and the Homeless* in which a sharp contrast is drawn between the fortunate poor and the utterly destitute poor such as the vagrant woman who, by implication, has lost through the ravages of war her husband, her home and her livelihood.

Faed's earliest genre paintings of Scottish rural life closely imitated Wilkie who had so memorably explored the principal theme of *Home and the Homeless* in his *Blind Fiddler* of 1806 (Tate Gallery, London). As in the case of Wilkie, Faed's most important pictures including *Home and Homeless* achieved wide circulation through the medium of reproductive engravings.

Robert Scott Lauder 1803–1869 · *Christ Teacheth Humility*

Oil on canvas,
237.8 × 353
Purchased by RAPFAS
1849; transferred to the
National Gallery 1897
NG 221

In its sheer scale and complexity, *Christ Teacheth Humility* represents the supreme effort of Lauder's career. Between 1838 and 1852 he was based in London where, in 1841, a select committee was formed to debate the promotion of the fine arts in relation to the reconstruction of the Houses of Parliament after their devastation by fire in 1834. The committee was succeeded by Royal Commission under the presidency of the Prince Consort which was dedicated to the promotion of epic narrative painting subsidised by the State, artists being selected through a series of highly publicised public competitions. For Lauder, as for Noel Paton and a number of their Scottish contemporaries, the prospect and prestige of State patronage for large-scale narrative painting proved irresistible.

After two years of intensive preparation, Lauder entered *Christ Walketh on the Sea* and *Christ Teacheth Humility* (Matthew:18) for the competition of 1847 and the related exhibition in Westminster Hall. His uncompromisingly painterly technique and richly coloured effects were opposed to the dry linear and fresco-like style preferred by the Commission and, although much admired, neither picture secured a premium. In its general conception and treatment *Christ Teacheth Humility* recalled Wilkie's unfinished *Knox Dispensing the Sacrament at Calder House*. The intrinsic merits of Lauder's rejected competition submission and its Scottish lineage were recognised by the Royal Association for the Promotion of the Fine Arts in Scotland. In 1849 the picture was purchased as a foundation work to be deposited in the future National Gallery of Scotland. Three years later Lauder returned to his native Edinburgh as the last and most influential of all the masters of the Trustees' Academy. His students in the rising generation included Orchardson, Pettie, McTaggart, Herdman and Graham.

William Fettes Douglas 1822–1891 · *The Spell* 1864

Remarkably, in view of his later pre-eminence in the Edinburgh art establishment, Fettes Douglas received no formal art training other than part-time tuition under Sir William Allan at the Trustees' Academy. In 1848 the former bank clerk formed The Smashers sketching club together with the brothers Faed and John Ballantyne. By 1854 Fettes Douglas was an Academician of the Royal Scottish Academy of which he was to hold the presidency from 1882 after serving as curator of the National Gallery of Scotland from 1877.

Fettes Douglas, Noel Paton and James Drummond were all prominent members of the Society of Antiquaries of Scotland, bibliophiles, and avid collectors of armour and Scottish antiquities. Fettes Douglas's private erudition was of a particularly esoteric nature, his preoccupation with alchemy, mysticism and Rosicrucianism being unparalleled among his Scottish contemporaries with the exception of David Scott. In *The Spell* a magician is portrayed endeavouring to raise the spirit of a dead man. As in so many of Fettes Douglas's compositions, the cluttered still life of books is invested with a surreal quality of independent existence. The ambience of the picture is further enhanced by an intensely expressive use of vacant space and by the distant view through the window embrasure of moonlit water and ancient standing stones.

In 1864 *The Spell* was immediately purchased from the Academy's exhibition by the Royal Association for the Promotion of Fine Arts in Scotland. By 1867 the picture had passed to the Dundonian collector G.B. Simpson, who also owned *The Legend* by Chalmers and *Spring* by McTaggart. Following its presentation to the Gallery in 1886, *The Spell* became an established favourite with public copyists.

Oil on canvas, 77.5 × 157
Presented by James T. Gibson-Craig 1886
NG 779

Sir Joseph Noel Paton 1821–1901 · The Quarrel of Oberon and Titania

Oil on canvas, 99 × 152
Purchased by RAPFAS
1850; transferred to the
National Gallery 1897
NG 293

As a distinctive and occasionally sub-versive sub-class of Victorian literary narrative painting, fairy painting afforded many alluring possibilities for escapism from the pressures of an in-dustrialised society, including the con-trolled exploration of the supernatural and the sanitised indulgence of sexual fantasies. In 1846 Paton exhibited his first exercise in this fashionable genre, a smaller version of The Quarrel of Oberon and Titania, which was deposited with the Royal Scottish Academy as his di-ploma work on his election as an Asso-ciate. The following year its pendant, The Reconciliation, was awarded a pre-mium in the prestigious public compe-tition for the decoration of the new Houses of Parliament. State-sponsored promotion of Shakespearian illustra-tion provided the perfect vehicle for large-scale fairy painting through the choice of A Midsummer Night's Dream and a specific episode which could also be interpreted as an allegory of harmonious government and a prosperous kingdom.

The King of Belgium was pre-empted in his desire to purchase The Reconciliation by the Royal Scottish Academy which had already secured it for the embryonic national collection of Scottish art. En-couraged by these accolades, Paton ex-hibited the present larger version of The Quarrel in Edinburgh in 1850 when it was judged to be the picture of the season and acquired by the Royal Association for the Promotion of Fine Arts in Scot-land. In 1857, while The Quarrel was on view in the partially completed National Gallery of Scotland, an enraptured Lewis Carroll counted one hundred and sixty five fairies in Paton's microscopically detailed Shakespearian microcosm.

Alexander Munro 1825–1871 · *Young Romilly*

The son of an Inverness dyer, Munro attracted the attention of Harriet, Duchess of Sutherland through his schoolboy ventures in portraiture and modelling in clay. At the invitation of Charles Barry, whom the duchess had engaged as supervising architect for the reconstruction of Dunrobin Castle, Munro moved to London in 1848 to work on the sculptural decoration of the new Houses of Parliament designed by Barry. While studying at the Royal Academy Schools, Munro was drawn into the social circle of Dante Gabriel Rossetti, Millais and other members of the future Pre-Raphaelite Brotherhood. From 1852 to 1858 Munro shared both his house and his studio with the painter Arthur Hughes.

Exhibited at the Royal Academy in 1863, this rare narrative sculpture is related to the literary figure groups with which Munro began to experiment in 1851. During the 1840s he had travelled extensively in the north of England. His immediate source for the present group was Wordsworth's poem *The Force of Prayer* which recounts the legend of the founding of Bolton Abbey in Yorkshire in memory of William of Egremont or 'Young Romilly'. Munro selected the moment of greatest dramatic tension when William and his greyhound are poised on the brink of the chasm into which they will plunge to their deaths in the River Wharfe. The sculptor's model was one of the younger sons of Herbert Ingram, founder of the *Illustrated London News*, in whose honour Munro carved the Ingram coat of arms on young Romilly's tunic.

Marble, h.97
Purchased 1993
NG 2571

William Bell Scott 1811–1890 · The Nativity 1872

Oil on canvas, 74 × 114
Purchased 1980
NG 2396

In 1859, while Master of the Government School of Design in Newcastle-upon-Tyne, Scott was introduced to Alice Boyd, herself an aspiring painter with local industrial connections. Following Scott's first visit to the Boyd family home at Penkill Castle in 1860, his emotional intimacy with Alice Boyd developed and, from the mid-1860s, Scott and his wife regularly spent the summers in Ayrshire with her in a discreet ménage à trois. In 1865, on the death of Alice Boyd's brother Spencer, who had restored Penkill, Scott painted an important series of murals in the castle staircase, illustrating the love poem *The Kingis Quair* composed by James I of Scotland.

Painted at Penkill, *The Nativity* formed part of Alice Boyd's extensive private collection. Scott himself was not an overtly practising Christian. His most unusual *Nativity* probably originated in his desire to paint as its setting a picturesque, tumbledown barn in the vicinity of Penkill at the insistent urging of Dante Gabriel Rossetti, a personal friend since the 1840s, who visited Penkill in 1869. Prototypes for Scott's compositional amalgamation of a modern setting with a New Testament subject were to be found in Pre-Raphaelite paintings of the 1850s and Scott's compatriot William Dyce had memorably employed Scottish landscapes in his *Man of Sorrows* and *David in the Wilderness* of about 1860. Begun in August 1871, Scott's *Nativity* is set in high summer and combines the separate episodes of the Adoration of the Shepherds and the Journey of the Magi.

William McTaggart 1835–1910 · *Spring* 1864

In 1863 the Dundonian textile manufacturer and collector G.B. Simpson commissioned from the young McTaggart a pair of pictures entitled *Spring* and *Autumn* (now in a private Scottish collection). As an amateur artist himself, Simpson proved to be an exacting but committed patron, advising McTaggart assiduously throughout the evolution of both compositions.

The essential and pre-existing idea for *Spring* was entirely of McTaggart's own invention. According to his usual procedure during the early 1860s, it was then developed through his pencil drawings and a compositional sketch in oils which was submitted as a test piece to the potential buyer for final approval or amendment. Simpson's dialogue with McTaggart was conducted by letter throughout 1863. In

1864 Simpson insisted on acquiring both the finished pictures *Spring* and *Autumn*, and the compositional sketches in his determination that no other collectors, especially his business associates, should have any stake in his McTaggart pictures.

Although the vivid green of the meadow in *Spring* was probably influenced by Pre-Raphaelite colour schemes, the picture as a whole was very un-Pre-Raphaelite in its purpose. McTaggart's lifelong preoccupation was the physical, atmospheric and emotional integration of figures into landscape with the aim of creating a complete unity of feeling. In *Spring* and *Autumn* his quest was pursued through the discreetly symbolic representation of childhood innocence, implicitly contrasted with the complexity and sadness of adult life.

Oil on canvas, 45.1 × 60.4
Bequest of Sir James Lewis Caw 1951
NG 2137

Robert Herdman 1829–1888 · A Riverbank at Corrie, Arran 1866

Watercolour and bodycolour on paper, 34.2 × 50.4
Purchased 1978
D 5049

Of the group of exceptionally gifted students to study under Robert Scott Lauder at Edinburgh's Trustees' Academy, Herdman was perhaps most attuned to his master's style and tastes. While a number of his class-mates migrated to London, Herdman, together with McTaggart and George Paul Chalmers, elected to settle in Edinburgh, where he established himself as a painter of portraits, Scottish genre and historical subjects. Inspired by Lauder's enthusiasm for the Venetian colourists, Herdman's works are distinguished by a rich and attractive colouring and painterly treatment.

From 1864 until the end of his life, Herdman made repeated trips to Arran, the most southerly of Scot-land's islands, renowned for its varied and breathtaking geology. Accompa-nied by his family, the artist spent long happy holidays at the seaside village of Corrie. Linked by ferries to the mainland ports of Gourock and Ardrossan, Corrie provided a conven-ient base from which to explore

Arran's granite peaks. The island also attracted a number of Herdman's friends and contemporaries including William Dyce, Chalmers and Joseph Noel Paton. In its subject, composition and careful observation of nature, this beautiful description of a boulder-strewn tributary, vegetated by fern and heather, and backed in the upper right corner by a purple-hued mountain slope, suggests Herdman's familiarity with John Ruskin's 1857 watercolour *In the Pass of Killiecrankie* (Fitzwilliam Museum, Cambridge).

Peter Graham 1836–1921 · *Wandering Shadows 1878*

A contemporary of Pettie, Orchardson and McTaggart, Graham was one of the brilliant generation of Scottish painters who trained under Robert Scott Lauder at the Trustees' Academy in Edinburgh during the early 1850s. Although Graham's first exhibited pictures were figure subjects, he turned to landscape in 1859 while on holiday in Deeside. In 1863 his six-foot picture, *In the Highlands*, caused a sensation at the Royal Scottish Academy's annual exhibition. Spurred on by his sudden local fame, Graham joined Pettie, Orchardson and the Faeds in London to take on the challenge of the Royal Academy.

In 1866 he rose to that challenge with *Spate in the Highlands* (Manchester City Art Gallery), a grandiose and emotionally charged study of the destructive fury of a Highland river in full flood. Although based on close and sensitive observation of fleeting effects in nature, Graham's transforming visions of the Highland landscape epitomised the representation of Scotland as the 'land of the mountain and the flood' at its most spectacular and technically virtuosic. Graham's essential formula owed as much to the enterprise of Horatio McCulloch as to the poetry of Sir Walter Scott and his own commercial potential was immediately recognised. From 1866 Graham exhibited only intermittently in Scotland. Painted on a scale commensurate with the grandeur of his interpretation, his great series of Highland landscapes was directed towards an urban London-based or London-oriented international audience.

Oil on canvas,
134.6 × 182.9
Purchased with the aid of Cowan Smith Bequest Fund
1944
NG 1986

John Phillip 1817–1867 · La Gloria: A Spanish Wake 1864

Oil on canvas,
145.4 × 219.2
Purchased with a
contribution from John
Ritchie Findlay 1897
NG 836

During the 1830s and 1840s, at the outset of a promising career divided between Aberdeen and London, Phillip explored the inheritance of Wilkie by dedicating himself to rural Scottish domestic genre in paintings such as *Presbyterian Catechising* of 1847 (in the Gallery's collection). In 1851 a recuperative visit to Spain changed the entire course of his career. Phillip's brilliant studies of Spanish life and character were commended by Landseer to Queen Victoria who purchased the *Spanish Gypsy Mother* as a Christmas gift for the Prince Consort. Two further extended visits to Spain were to confirm the artist in his new self-appointed identity as 'Spanish' Phillip.

The first significant British painter of his generation to visit Spain in the late 1820s was Wilkie who revelled in this 'wild unpoached game reserve of Europe'. Wilkie had been followed by Roberts and J.F. Lewis in 1832 and William Allan in 1834. The major subject pictures arising from Phillip's final Spanish sojourn in 1860, in particular *La Gloria* and the unfinished *Spanish Boys Playing at Bullfighting*, transformed in spectacular fashion the conventions of this earlier Scottish Mediterranean Orientalism by presenting genre on a scale tradition-ally reserved for epic narrative painting. In *La Gloria*, which Phillip himself considered his masterpiece, he portrayed the Spanish, as distinct from Scottish, observance of the 'wake' or vigil and lamentation over the deceased. The mother, in the shadowed zone on the left, is isolated in her mourning for her dead baby while the bystanders celebrate the passing of the innocent child whose soul is presumed to have flown straight to heaven.

Sir William Quiller Orchardson 1832–1910 · *Master Baby* 1886

In 1862 Orchardson joined the dispersal of brilliant students of Robert Scott Lauder by migrating to London where he shared a house with Tom Graham and John Pettie. Orchardson's marriage to Ellen Moxon in 1873 inspired some of his most memorable, intimate and incisive experiments with portraiture including the full-length of his bride-to-be in the Gallery's collection. Lady Orchardson and her baby son Gordon were the models for this strikingly unsentimental and monumental reinterpretation of the motif of mother and child so beloved of the artist's contemporaries among the later Victorian domestic genre painters.

Although based on an actual incident, Orchardson's design was constructed with immense care. The creative process of synthesis and simplification, assisted by the artist's obvious familiarity with the compositional conventions of the woodcuts of the great Japanese printmaker Utamaro, can be traced through his detailed preparatory drawings of which several are held by the Gallery. In 1886 the finished picture was shown at the Grosvenor Gallery, the principal London venue for the promotion of avant garde British painting. Admired by Sickert, the critic and novelist George Moore, and by Degas, a committed devotee of Orchardson, *Master Baby* generated through its public exhibition a number of imitative compositions by younger or less inventive artists. Two such examples are, *Mother and her Child* (National Gallery of Victoria, Melbourne), exhibited by John Longstaff at the Paris Salon in 1891, and *Motherhood* (Art Gallery of South Australia, Adelaide), painted in London in 1902 by George Coates.

Oil on canvas, 109 × 168
Purchased with the aid of an anonymous donor 1913
NG 1138

William York MacGregor 1855–1923 · *The Vegetable Stall* 1884

Oil on canvas, 106.7 × 153
Presented by Mrs William
York MacGregor 1939
NG 1915

At the beginning of the 1880s the loose-knit brotherhood of young radicals dubbed the Glasgow Boys, and including MacGregor's long-standing friend James Paterson, regularly congregated in MacGregor's studio in Bath Street, Glasgow, to receive instruction and exchange pictorial ideas. To an extent MacGregor's masterpiece, completed in 1884, epitomised the shared ideal for which the Glasgow Boys were then striving; a bold, vigorous, painterly grasp of Francophile realism.

Years later Stanley Cursiter, an artist and Director of the National Galleries of Scotland during the 1930s and 1940s, recalled Oskar Kokoschka's astounded reaction to *The Vegetable Stall*: 'To think that the picture was painted before I was born – and I never knew!' Kokoschka recognised and was elated by the quasi-abstract monumentality of MacGregor's treatment of his still-life subject, without precedent or succession within the productions of the Glasgow School. Yet the picture was not originally conceived within the format of pure still-life painting which so impressed Kokoschka. In 1984 an X-ray examination revealed, amongst other pentimenti, the figure of a girl at the right-hand side of the canvas; a street trader counting the takings of her market stall. Had MacGregor not painted out this figure for reasons unknown, his picture would have been appraised as a remarkable figurative composition to be measured against comparable works by Jules Bastien-Lepage, William Stott of Oldham and James Guthrie.

James Paterson 1854–1932 · *Autumn in Glencairn, Moniaive 1887*

Unlike the majority of the Glasgow Boys, Paterson was primarily a landscape painter for whom figures were only of incidental significance. Yet, from the outset, he was widely recognised as being one of the dominant figures of the Glasgow School, both for his contribution as a landscape painter and as chief promoter of *The Scottish Art Review*, launched as the Glasgow Boys' literary and ideological journal in 1888. The first of the group to study in France, Paterson returned annually to the Paris ateliers until 1883.

His closest associate in Glasgow and regular painting companion for summer excursions to Fife and the north east of Scotland was W.Y. MacGregor. From 1879 Paterson began to explore the alternative attractions of the Dumfriesshire village of Moniaive which was to become his permanent base in 1884, when he married, until his decisive move to Edinburgh in 1897. Far from being restrictive, this enduring commitment to Moniaive arose from his conviction that landscape painters should not 'flirt with a new neighbour each remaining summer but ... marry metaphysically some well-chosen space'. On its inaugural appearance at the Glasgow Institute in 1888, *Autumn in Glencairn, Moniaive*, was greeted as his most important and expressive Dumfriesshire landscape, invested with that special feeling of time and place which distinguished his finest work.

Oil on canvas, 102 × 127
Purchased with the aid of
the Barrogill Keith Bequest
Fund 1984
NG 2424

Sir James Guthrie 1859–1930 · *A Hind's Daughter* 1883

Oil on canvas, 91.5 × 76.2
Bequest of Sir James Lewis
Caw 1951
NG 2142

Essentially self-taught, Guthrie studied briefly in London with John Pettie, but rapidly jettisoned his shared interest in literary subject pictures. In 1879 Guthrie formed a group with E.A. Walton and Joseph Crawhall, painting landscapes *en plein air* at Rosneath on the Clyde coast. Guthrie's direct encounter with the work of Bastien-Lepage in Paris in 1882 confirmed his own commitment to plein-air naturalism and radically changed his outlook.

In 1883 Guthrie effectively assumed leadership of the extended community of plein-air landscape and figure painters who congregated at the Berwickshire village of Cockburnspath and were soon to acquire a collective identity as the Glasgow School. Whereas Walton, Crawhall, Henry and Melville were migratory summer visitors, Guthrie remained throughout the winter in Cockburnspath where he executed *A Hind's Daughter* in the solid, static, earth-coloured type of painting derived from Bastien-Lepage and the leading artists of the Hague School with typical square brushstrokes and square signature. In one sense Guthrie's subject-matter was, however, intensely and irreducibly Scottish. From the eighteenth century kail (or cabbage) had been the staple diet of the Scots cottagers and 'hinds' or farm labourers.

Edward Arthur Walton 1860–1922 · A Daydream 1885

During the early 1880s the Glasgow Boys' determination to evolve new forms of painting and to explore a distinctively Scottish type of rustic realism was reinforced by their exposure to the works of Millet and the painters of Barbizon School in the annual exhibitions of the Glasgow Institute and by the rising British reputation of Jules Bastien-Lepage. Of all the Glasgow Boys, Walton displayed a particular aptitude and a lasting preference for pure landscape painting in oils and in watercolours, a medium in which he excelled. From the mid-1880s to the 1890s he experimented with the integration of the human figure into landscape in a series of ambitious compositions from A Daydream to Bluette, painted about 1891, and also in the Gallery's collection.

Begun en plein air (out of doors) at Cockburnspath in Berwickshire, the Glasgow Boys' equivalent of Barbizon, A Daydream was completed in Helensburgh in 1885 and launched at the Glasgow Institute in 1887 as Walton's first attempt at a monumental exhibition picture. As one of the outstanding Glasgow School figurative paintings of the 1880s, A Daydream was included in the Walton Memorial Exhibition in Glasgow in 1924 where Walton's bold and massive treatment of his simple rustic figures and his resonant and subdued tonal range drew direct comparisons with the work of Bastien-Lepage.

Oil on canvas,
139.7 × 116.8
Purchased with the aid of
the National Art Collections
Fund 1999
NG 2702

Sir John Lavery 1856–1941

The Dutch Cocoa House at the Glasgow International Exhibition of 1888 · 1888

Oil on canvas, 45.8 × 35.7
Purchased with the aid of
the Barrogill Keith Bequest
Fund 1985
NG 2431

Lavery's endeavours as informal artist-in-residence at the Glasgow International Exhibition of 1888 were to contribute quite substantially to his success as a society portraitist in the 1890s. The exhibition was devised in a spirit of civic rivalry in an attempt to upstage both the 1887 Royal Jubilee Exhibition held by Manchester, a significant industrial competitor, and the 1886 International Exhibition staged by Glasgow's traditional adversary, the city of Edinburgh. In addition, in emulation of the Great Exhibition of 1851 at Crystal Palace, the Glasgow project was intended to fund the new art gallery and museum in Kelvingrove park and a municipal school of art on a scale commensurate with Glasgow's growing commercial and industrial stature.

The exhibition design, by the Glasgow architect James Sellars, was predominantly Oriental but eclectic in the extreme and provided Lavery with a seemingly endless supply of motifs. During the summer of 1888 he produced over fifty small oils depicting the military tattoo, the band concerts and the sideshows at 'Baghdad by Kelvinside' and culminating in a civic commission to record Queen Victoria's visit in a grand ceremonial group portrait (Glasgow Art Gallery and Museum). The Old Dutch House erected by the world-renowned cocoa manufacturers Van Houten & Son of Weesp near Amsterdam was situated in close proximity to the grand entrance and to the museum at Kelvingrove where the Royal Jubilee gifts were displayed. Lavery mounted a one-man show of his exhibition pictures at the Craibe Angus Gallery in Queen Street, Edinburgh, in October 1888.

Arthur Melville 1855–1904
An Arab Interior 1881

In 1878, after studying with James Campbell Noble, a successful Edinburgh painter of landscape and rustic genre, Melville migrated to Paris and thence to the artists' colony at Grez-sur-Loing where he settled in the spring of 1879. During this period of intensive familiarisation with contemporary French practice, Melville evolved the distinctive 'blottesque' technique which became a hallmark of his scintillating watercolours executed during the 1880s and 1890s and by which he is still best known.

In 1880, following the precedent of his Scottish predecessors Allan, Wilkie and Roberts, Melville embarked on an extended tour of the Near and Middle East, financed by the proceeds from the vigorous sales of his French works in Edinburgh. From Cairo he sailed to India before journeying home overland through Turkey and Eastern Europe. On returning to Scotland, he began to associate regularly with his radical Glasgow contemporaries, particularly Joseph Crawhall and James Guthrie. Worked up from sketches made in Cairo in 1881, *An Arab Interior* reflects in its low-keyed colour and emphasis on symphonic tonal harmony the French training so highly prized by Melville and by the young Glasgow Boys. His exploration of the complex possibilities of abstract pattern-making afforded by the Musharabeyah woodwork recalls the intricate structuring of the picturesque harem interiors painted by John Frederick Lewis, one of the most virtuosic of the later Victorian Orientalists.

Oil on canvas, 95 × 72.8
Bequest of Sir James Lewis Caw
NG 2144

Arthur Melville 1855–1904 · A Moorish Procession, Tangier 1893

Watercolour over pencil on paper, 59.3 × 79.8
Purchased 1907
D NG 947

Melville travelled to Tangier twice, firstly in the spring of 1890 and again in spring 1893. Both trips were combined with a tour of Spain, where he gathered material for the colourful bullfighting subjects of his later years. He was probably inspired to visit Morocco by his friend and fellow artist Joseph Crawhall, who had journeyed regularly to Tangier from about 1884 to 1893. The city's vibrant lifestyle and alluring exoticism, so different to the cultured bourgeois existence of much of Europe, attracted many nineteenth-century artists. By the 1880s Tangier supported a thriving community of British expatriates. Among Melville's generation to visit the city were several Glasgow Boys, including (in addition to Crawhall) Thomas Millie

Dow, John Lavery, Alexander Mann and William Kennedy.

Contemporary accounts confirm that it was Tangier's dazzling white light and brilliant colours, ever shifting with the passage of the baking sun, that made the deepest impression on visiting artists. In this virtuoso watercolour, Melville captures the atmospheric clamour of a local parade, its participants clad in hooded brown jellabs, moving to the noisy accompaniment of pipe and drum. The work demonstrates his masterly watercolour technique, dubbed 'blottesque' on account of his method of laying in primary accents in controlled spots and puddles of colour – a manner much copied by other British watercolourists.

Joseph Crawhall 1861–1913 · *The White Drake*

Though born in Northumbria, Crawhall is generally classified as a Scottish artist, due to his close association with the group of artists known as the Glasgow Boys, in particular James Guthrie, E.A. Walton and Arthur Melville. Together with the latter two, he is recognised as one of the group's most outstanding and innovative watercolourists.

Nicknamed affectionately 'Creeps', on account of his introvert and silent nature, Crawhall had since childhood taken pleasure in the undemanding companionship of animals. As a keen huntsman, horses and dogs rated highly amongst his favourite pictorial subjects, together with birds and other farmyard creatures. Unlike the many Victorian artists who produced cloying, sentimentalising pictures of domestic pets, Crawhall respected the individuality and nobility of animals. He worked primarily from memory, and would study his subjects intensely, before attempting to distil the essence of their form and character on paper or linen. In contrast to the blank backdrop that typifies many of Crawhall's bird studies, *The White Drake* is portrayed within a natural habitat of vibrant colours. The considered organisation of dandelions, daisies and reeds, coupled with the drake's simplified profile, creates a flattened perspective, contributing to the overall decorative quality of the composition. Attributes such as these reveal Crawhall's appreciation for Oriental art, particularly Japanese prints and Chinese wash drawings on silk.

Watercolour and gouache on linen, 40.7 × 57.1
Purchased with support from the National Lottery through the Heritage Lottery Fund, and the National Art Collections Fund 1996
D 5415

William McTaggart 1835–1910 · The Storm 1890

Oil on canvas, 122 × 183
Presented by Mrs Andrew
Carnegie 1935
NG 1834

In 1901, at the artist's request, the Edinburgh dealer Peter McOmish Dott toured an exhibition of thirty-two McTaggarts to Glasgow, Edinburgh and Dundee. This major selling exhibition was intended to raise funds for the ailing engineering business of McTaggart's eldest son. The highest price was secured for The Storm, purchased by Andrew Carnegie as a tour de force of McTaggart's landscape painting. In 1935, in commemoration of the dual centenary of the birth of the artist and of his patron, Carnegie's widow presented his finest McTaggart to the National Gallery of Scotland.

A smaller version of this composition (in Kirkcaldy Art Gallery) had been painted out of doors in 1883 at Carradale in Kintyre where McTaggart frequently spent the summer. In this first picture, which was much more tautly handled, the narrative content and the definition of the individual figures were more immediately conspicuous. In the 1890 picture, a studio production, the expressive capacities of fierce, energised brushwork and colour were realised to the full, the whole surface becoming a turbulent mesh of lashing wind and heaving water. Yet the human element still predominates in the form of the tiny endangered fishing vessel and the launching of a rescue boat by the anxious bystanders on the shore. McTaggart's subject is essentially the fragility and resilience of human resistance pitted against massive and violent forces.

George Henry 1858–1943 · *Geisha Girl* 1894

Oil on canvas, 53.3 × 32.8
Bequest of Alexander Esmé
Gordon 1993
NG 2583

At the Glasgow Art Club's grand costume ball in 1889 E.A. Walton appeared as the great Japanese printmaker Hokusai, the ultimate expression of Orientalist taste and aesthetics among the avant garde painters of the Glasgow School. In Glasgow the fashionable British preoccupation with all things Japanese had been stimulated by the staging of an ambitious exhibition of Oriental art in the Corporation Galleries in 1882, most of the exhibits consisting of artefacts presented to the city by the Japanese Government. Within the immediate circle of the Glasgow Boys, Grosvenor Thomas and James Paterson's art dealer brother formed a business partnership trading in Japanese curios.

In February 1893 Walton's contemporaries, George Henry and E. A. Hornel, who had developed a close friendship and artistic collaboration, set out on an extended tour of Japan. Their travels were part-funded by the Glasgow shipping magnate and collector William Burrell (founder of the Burrell Collection in Glasgow) and by the dealer Alexander Reid. In Henry's case the impact of this visit was momentous but relatively short-lived. The *Geisha Girl* is among the finest of his many compositions on this theme, painted in oil or in watercolours during the mid-1890s immediately after his return. Henry's fascination with the orchestration of surface pattern was intensified by his direct encounter with Japanese art. Here the decorative effect is enlivened by a perfectly controlled use of jewel-like notes of vibrant colour.

Edward Atkinson Hornel 1864–1933 · The Music of the Woods 1906

Following the triumphant exhibition of his Japanese subject pictures at Alexander Reid's gallery in Glasgow in 1895, Hornel embarked on a long self-imposed exile in Kirkudbright, gradually distancing himself from George Henry and his other close associates among the Glasgow School. From the late 1890s he reverted to the highly decorative and brilliantly colouristic compositions of young girls in the Galloway countryside with which he had begun to court popularity and occasional critical controversy at the beginning of the decade. By the turn of the century pictures of this type were being eagerly acquired for many public and private collections throughout Britain and even overseas. A masterpiece in the artist's own estimation, *The Music of the Woods* was secured by the Scottish collector Sir Hugh Reid immediately on comple-tion. In 1907 the Royal Academy, unanimously but vainly, advocated the purchase of the picture for the national collection of British art at the Tate Gallery.

Public demand for this type of Hornel is now almost as vigorous as it was in the early 1900s despite his marked decline into mannerism and formulaic self-repetition during the last two decades of his career. Increasing commercial success enabled Hornel to purchase outright the Georgian mansion of Broughton House in Kirkudbright, now vested in the National Trust for Scotland. In 1933 he bequeathed to the town of Kirkudbright, as his adoptive home since early childhood, the house and its Japanese-style garden together with the contents of his studio which included the most representative collection of his paintings.

Oil on canvas, 121 × 151.1
Presented by Sir Hugh Reid
1934
NG 1814

In 1936 the Gallery accepted from the artist's estate a bequest totalling eleven works by Phoebe Anna Traquair who, in 1920, had become the first woman to obtain membership of the Royal Scottish Academy. She had settled in Edinburgh in 1874 after leaving her native Dublin on her marriage to Dr Ramsay Traquair, Keeper of Natural History at the Royal Scottish Museum. A correspondent or friend of Ruskin, Holman Hunt, W.B.Yeats and the Scottish architect Robert Lorimer, Traquair achieved international recognition as one of the most versatile and accomplished figures in the Arts and Crafts movement and the Scottish cultural renaissance of the early twentieth century. A committed exponent of the indivisibility of the arts, she explored an exceptionally wide variety of media including large-scale mural decoration, easel painting, book illumination, enamel jewellery, and embroidery.

Her magnificent suite of four embroideries entitled *The Progress of a Soul* was conceived in 1893, the first to be completed being *The Entrance* in 1895 and the last, *The Victory*, in 1902. The central figure was loosely based on the character Denys L'Auxerrois from *Imaginary Portraits* by Walter Pater, the influential English critic and writer whose aesthetic philosophy had shaped the doctrine of 'Art for Art's Sake'. Traquair's reincarnation of Pater's Denys represented the spirit of man. In the opening panel the blissful human soul is still in the 'happy stage of hope and enthusiasm, innocence and ignorance of the realities of life'. While engaged on the second panel *The Stress*, Traquair developed the idea of the spiritual odyssey within an explicitly Christian context through a mural decoration of the *Parable of the Ten Virgins* painted for the Catholic Apostolic church in East London Street, Edinburgh.

Silk and gold thread embroidered on linen, 180.7 × 71.2
Bequest of the artist 1936
NG 1865 A

John Duncan 1866–1945 · *Saint Bride* 1913

Tempera on canvas,
122.3 × 144.5
Purchased 1946
NG 2043

Duncan was one of the most eclectic and idiosyncratic Scottish artists associated with the Celtic Revival movement which encompassed both visual arts and literature during the 1890s and in Edinburgh derived its guiding inspiration from the philosophy and aesthetics of Sir Patrick Geddes. Steeped in the study of early Italian fresco painting, Duncan familiarised himself with experimental techniques of tempera then widely practised by his own contemporaries among the mural painters of France. He amalgamated the flattened linear forms of the Renaissance and the modern tradition with the spirals and interlaces of Celtic design to create a distinctive style which was deliberately dreamlike and otherworldly.

The assimilation of the Celtic goddess Brigid or Bride into Christian tradition began in the fifth or sixth century AD through the historical Saint Bride who supposedly founded a religious community at Kildare. According to legend, the Irish saint, popularly known as 'Mary of the Gael' and the 'Foster-Mother of Christ', was miraculously transported to Bethlehem to be present at the nativity of Christ. Duncan's individualistic presentation of this legend reflects his fascination with the landscape of the Outer Hebrides and the Isle of Iona, the symbolic or actual setting of so many of his interpretations of Celtic myth. The tiny clown accompanying the procession of the Magi on the leading angel's robe is thought to be a self-portrait of the artist who may have cast himself as a holy fool, a concept primarily but not exclusively associated with Christian tradition.

David Gauld 1865–1936 · *Saint Agnes*

Oil on canvas 61.3 × 35.8
Purchased with the aid of
the National Art Collections
Fund 1999
NG 2585

From the mid-1890s Gauld was almost exclusively identified with the ruralist paintings of Ayrshire calves whose immense popularity has continued to eclipse his more innovatory achievements as a decorative artist. After studying part-time at Glasgow School of Art as a friend and a contemporary of Charles Rennie Mackintosh, Gauld first attracted attention during the late 1880s with his illustrations to the *Glasgow Weekly Citizen* which reflected the current vogue for Japanese prints. In the subject-matter of his early easel paintings, including *Saint Agnes*, and in the conception of his ecclesiastical and domestic stained glass designs, Gauld was strongly influenced by the Symbolism of Rossetti and Burne-Jones.

The selection of *Saint Agnes* for the triumphant showing of the Glasgow Boys at the Munich International Exhibition of 1890 highlighted the enduring significance of the picture as an extraordinary anticipation of Art Nouveau. The exceptional quality and importance of *Saint Agnes* was immediately recognised by the most influential promoter of the Glasgow School, the dealer Alexander Reid, who purchased it privately on the closure of the Munich exhibition. Following upon the Gallery's acquisition of *Saint Agnes* in 1999, *Music* – another emblematic and exactly contemporary composition – was presented to the Hunterian Art Gallery in Glasgow. The radical experimentalism of these two early easel paintings, was to remain unequalled in the history of the Glasgow School.

Robert Burns 1869–1941 · *Diana and her Nymphs*

From the 1920s the vast majority of Burns's commercial designs were commissioned by the Crawford dynasty of bakers and biscuit manufacturers or by one of their many business associates. In 1923 David Crawford's expansion of the family enterprise resulted in a remarkable commission to provide a complete decorative scheme for his exclusive tea rooms at 70 Princes Street, Edinburgh. Of its type this scheme was unparalleled in Scotland since the Willow Tea Rooms in Sauchiehall Street and the Ingram Street Tea Rooms had been fitted out by Charles Rennie Mackintosh for the Glasgow restaurateur Miss Cranston over a decade earlier. In order to achieve the 'unity and coherence' which Crawford stipulated, Burns co-ordinated every aspect of the interior design from the murals to the cake-stands and the music programmes for the resident orchestra.

This spectacular panel was installed on the first floor of the premises, just off the stairs. The decor originally incorporated four highly stylised representations of Greek goddesses. Despite the classical subject, the vibrant colour and zig-zag patterns of the Diana panel endow it with a rhythmic energy and excitement which is wholly of the 1920s. In an unexpected touch of whimsicality the small green car was introduced as a humorous reference to the artist's passion for motoring. The central figure was later adapted as a biscuit tin label for William Crawford and Sons, the senior branch of the dynasty.

Oil or tempera on canvas,
198.1 × 198.1
Purchased 1987
NG 2450

Sir David Young Cameron 1865–1945 · The Hill of the Winds

Oil on canvas,
116.8 × 132.7
Bequest of Robert Younger,
Baron Blanesburgh 1947
NG 2080

From the late 1880s Cameron exhibited regularly in London and Edinburgh both as a painter and as an etcher and with the Secessionists in Berlin and Munich. As an etcher, he was naturally predisposed to emphasise rich tonal contrasts in his oil paintings which are characterised by strong linear design combined with areas of massed and deep shadow. In all his chosen media Cameron's landscapes, which account for over half of his total production of original prints, display an extraordinary austerity and often exude a sense of desolation or spiritual remoteness. Although he preferred exactly the same type of mountain scenery as Horatio McCulloch, he rejected, in his own visions of the hills, the glamour and emotional accessibility of the McCulloch tradition of landscape painting. First exhibited in 1913, *The Hill of the Winds* is an imposing example of Cameron's landscapes in which natural forms are pared and refined down to quintessentials, suggesting something very primitive, elemental and alien.

In his own original printmaking, Cameron's ultimate inspiration was Rembrandt, arguably the greatest of all the Old Master painter-etchers. Cameron built up a superb private collection of Rembrandt etchings, many acquired from Colnaghi's in part payment for his own plates. This collection, together with his modern bronzes and a substantial sum of money for acquisitions, was bequeathed to the National Gallery of Scotland of which he had served as a trustee for twenty-five years.

Paul Sandby 1731–1809 · Horse Fair on Bruntsfield Links, Edinburgh 1750

Paul Sandby achieved distinction for his prodigious output of topographical and picturesque landscapes in watercolour, gouache and aquatint. Like his older brother, Thomas, he began his career with the Board of Ordnance in London. Shortly after his employment, around 1746, he was appointed chief draughtsman to the Military Survey in Scotland, based in Edinburgh.

Sandby spent about five years in Scotland, during which time he travelled and charted extensive tracts of the country. In addition to producing maps and topographical drawings, he delighted in sketching the lives and characters of the Scottish populace. This sheet was probably composed from recollections of Edinburgh's All-Hallows fair, an event held annually during the first week of November. Sandby sets his reconstruction on the Boroughmuir, an expanse of common land to the south-west of the city. His amusing examination of the social gathering highlights the plentiful supply of alcohol, which occasioned high spirits and numerous drunken scuffles. The scene revolves around two beer tents, which may be identified by their symbols (horns and a tail, and a leafy bough) as belonging to the well-known Edinburgh taverns The Black Bull and The Green Tree. Several town guard, armed with Lochaber axes, patrol wearily through the jovial crowd in the middle distance.

Watercolour over pencil on paper, 24.4 × 37.4
Purchased by Private Treaty
1990
D 5184

Thomas Gainsborough 1727–1788 · *The Honourable Mrs Graham (1757–1792)*

Oil on canvas, 237 × 154
Bequest of Robert Graham of
Redgorton 1859
NG 332

An acclaimed exhibit at the Royal Academy in 1777, Gainsborough's 'compleatest of all pictures' portrays the Honourable Mary Cathcart, daughter of 9th Baron Cathcart, Ambassador-Extraordinary to Catherine the Great. Sittings for the picture – one of at least three Gainsborough portraits of this exquisite society beauty – began in 1775, the year after her marriage to the Perthshire laird Thomas Graham, later Lord Lynedoch. The costume and accessories chosen for this portrait, arguably the grandest of all Gainsborough's full-lengths in the Van Dyck tradition, deliberately recalled the Rubens of Helena (or Suzanne) Fourment which is now in the Calouste Gulbenkian Foundation in Lisbon. The purchase of the Rubens as a Van Dyck by the Prime Minister, Sir Robert Walpole, in the early eighteenth century inspired numerous imitative adaptations in British portraiture from the 1730s to the 1780s.

Mary Cathcart's premature death in 1792 left her husband devastated. From 1794, when he raised the Perthshire Volunteers, Graham sought distraction through an army career and was promoted to general after serving with Wellington in the Peninsula. Unable to endure contemplation of his late wife's portrait, Graham lent it to her sister the Countess of Mansfield for Kenwood House in Hampstead before consigning it to the custody of a London art dealer. Years later the Gainsborough was rediscovered in storage by Graham's heir who left it to the newly opened Gallery in 1859 on condition that the picture should never leave Scotland.

Sir Joshua Reynolds 1723–1792 · *The Ladies Waldegrave*

Lady Charlotte Maria Waldegrave, later Countess of Euston and Duchess of Grafton (1761–1808); Lady Elizabeth Laura Waldegrave, later Countess Waldegrave (1760–1816); and Lady Anna Horatia Waldegrave, later Lady Seymour (1762–1801)

Oil on canvas, 143 × 168.3
Purchased with the aid of
the National Art Collections
Fund 1952
NG 2171

At the Royal Academy exhibition of 1781 Horace Walpole reported with gratification that his most recent commission to Reynolds was 'a most beautiful composition; the pictures very like and the attitudes natural and easy'. Antiquarian, connoisseur-collector and arbiter of taste, Walpole had already commissioned two portraits of himself from Reynolds for his showpiece Gothic Revival villa, Strawberry Hill, in Twickenham, west London. In the absence of their mother, the re-married widow of the 2nd Earl Waldegrave, the three beautiful Waldegrave sisters spent much time with their great-uncle at Strawberry Hill. In 1780, at Walpole's request, they sat to Reynolds for this imposingly monumental yet intimate conversation piece.

Walpole himself, despite his personal friendship for the artist, had little sympathy with Sir Joshua's advocacy of the Grand Manner in which he sought to enhance the status of the art of portraiture by assimilating canonical poses adapted from Old Master painting or classical sculpture. In Walpole's commissioned picture any predictable allusion to the Three Graces has been subordinated to a refreshing naturalism. The three ladies Waldegrave are united within the picture space by participation in a communal activity, a simple compositional device which complements perfectly their actual blood relationship in life. On the right, Lady Anna Horatia is using a hook to make lace on the net held by her tambour frame while Lady Charlotte Maria holds the skein of silk which the eldest sister Lady Elizabeth Laura is winding on to a card.

Thomas Girtin 1775–1802 · *The Village of Jedburgh, Roxburgh 1800*

Watercolour over pencil on paper, 30.2 × 52.1
Purchased with the aid of funds from the National Heritage Memorial Fund, the National Art Collections Fund and the Pilgrim Trust 1988
D 5175

Girtin made only one trip to Scotland, in 1796, when he combined a sketching expedition to northern England with a brief circuit through the Borders. Jedburgh and its ruined mediaeval abbey, situated on the banks of the Jed Water in Teviotdale, inspired several finished watercolours of which this is the last and the greatest. Based on a pencil sketch, now in the British Museum, London, the town is viewed from the elevated site of the former Jedburgh Castle, looking in a northerly direction. Girtin elects to omit the venerable relic of Jedburgh Abbey, which stands to the right of the area contained by his composition. The broad street, flanked by modest thatched cottages, vanishes rapidly into the middle distance, from where the eye is allowed to wander across the Jed's broad flood-plain to the rolling hills beyond. Plumes of smoke drift gently in the still air, enhancing the scene's tranquil atmosphere.

Girtin was an exact contemporary and friend of Joseph Mallord William Turner, with whom he headed the development of watercolour painting, from a lowly medium reserved for the humble art of topography, to one capable of rivalling oils in visual impact and emotional range. At his death, aged only twenty-seven, he was acknowledged alongside Turner as a leader of the modern British landscape school.

Joseph Mallord William Turner 1775–1851 · *The Piazzetta, Venice*

This is one of thirty-eight drawings and watercolours by Turner which were bequeathed to the Gallery in 1900 by the London collector and connoisseur, Sir Henry Vaughan. The group contains works from various periods and projects throughout Turner's career, and displays his consummate mastery of the watercolour medium. In compliance with the terms of the bequest, the collection is exhibited only once a year, during the month of January, when the daylight is at its weakest and least destructive levels.

Turner visited Venice on three occasions, in 1819, 1833 and 1840. He made over 170 watercolour sketches of the city, of which Vaughan owned nine. Six of these are now in the National Gallery of Scotland, and three in the National Gallery of Ireland, Dublin. Watermarked with the date 1834, this sheet numbers among the most spectacular of Turner's Venetian studies. The Piazzetta is here pictured from the waterfront of the Bacino di San Marco, looking towards the Palazzo Ducale, with the Marciana Library to the left. Two monolithic granite columns, one crowned with a winged lion, the symbol of St Mark, and the other with an effigy of St Theodore, the first patron saint of Venice, stand prominent in the foreground. A bolt of lightning, scratched from the surface of the paper, illuminates the surrounding architecture, revealing the façade and one dome of the Basilica di San Marco behind.

Watercolour and bodycolour, with pen and ink and scraping out on paper, 22.1 × 32.1

Henry Vaughan Bequest 1900

D NG 871

William Blake 1757–1827 · God Writing upon the Tables of the Covenant

Pen and ink, and
watercolour over pencil on
paper, 41.9 × 34.2
William Findlay Watson
Bequest 1881
D 2281

Printmaker, painter, poet and mystic
philosopher, Blake is today celebrated
as one of the greatest imaginative
artists of the British School. An early
apprenticeship to the engraver James
Basire equipped him with the skills
that were to support him for much of
his life, and enabled him to develop a
unique method of 'illuminated
printing' in which he married text and
image. Alongside his prolific
printmaking activities, Blake created
numerous works in tempera and
watercolour. This composition
belongs to a group of eighty watercolours of biblical subjects, produced
between 1800 to around 1809, for one
of Blake's most loyal patrons, Thomas
Butts.

Remnants of an inscription on the
original mount reveal that the
inspiration for this watercolour came
from the Old Testament (Deuter-
onomy 9:10). The statuesque figure of
Jehovah, clad in diaphanous robes,
stands amid the fire of an assembly of
trumpeting angels, his arms raised
and finger poised in readiness to
inscribe the Ten Commandments on
the stone tablets borne before him.
Moses, diminutive in size, bows in
worship beneath the Lord's feet. The
symmetrical design and linear, almost
neoclassical sculpting of form,
suggests that the work was executed
around 1805. Another watercolour
from this series, *Job Confessing his
Presumption to God who Answers from the
Whirlwind*, is also in the Gallery's
collection.

John Martin 1789–1854 · *Macbeth*

In 1820 Martin exhibited at the British Institution in London a substantially larger (and now unlocated) version of the Gallery's picture, depicting the climactic encounter on the blasted heath between Macbeth, Banquo and the weird sisters who predict Macbeth's violent accession as King of Scots (*Macbeth*, act I, scene III). Evidently painted as an independent speculation, the picture remained Martin's unique venture in Shakespearian illlustration.

In 1786 Alderman John Boydell, later Lord Mayor of London, had established his commercial Shakespeare Gallery in Pall Mall to promote British history painting through the medium of Shakespearian illustration. The apocalyptic conception and romantic idiom, if not the scale, of Martin's *Macbeth* differed radically from most of these earlier Boydell-commissioned productions. The theatricality of Martin's composition is of a cosmic order in which the turbulent skies and exaggerated forms of the mountainous landscape become an extended metaphor for the impending cataclysm which will engulf the entire Scottish nation. In representing eleventh-century Scottish costume, however, Martin aspired, paradoxically, towards historical authenticity. For the Highland dress worn by Macbeth and Banquo, he sought advice from the brothers Sobieski Stuart as self-appointed authorities on historical costume and presumed descendants of Prince Charles Edward Stewart.

By 1831 the exhibited version of *Macbeth* had still not found a purchaser. That year it was seen in Martin's studio by Sir Walter Scott who lamented his inability to afford the picture for Abbotsford.

Oil on canvas 50.1 × 71
Purchased 1949
NG 2115

John Constable 1776–1837 · *The Vale of Dedham*

Oil on canvas, 144.5 × 122
Purchased with the aid of
the National Art Collections
Fund 1944
NG 2016

Among his British contemporaries, including his great rival J.M.W. Turner, Constable was exceptional in never venturing overseas and remaining passionately committed to the intensive observation and celebration of the fertile countryside within a few miles radius of his native village of East Bergholt in Suffolk. For the Royal Academy exhibition of 1828 and his 'best' picture, his passport to election as an Academician in 1829, Constable resolved on the definitive treatment of a subject which had preoccupied him for over twenty years – the view from Gun Hill (now called Langham Coombe), looking down the Stour valley towards the church at Dedham, where his father worked a watermill, and beyond towards Harwich and the Stour estuary.

In 1802, when he had first dedicated himself to 'natural painture', Constable had painted a smaller upright landscape from an identical viewpoint (Victoria and Albert Museum, London). Yet his credo of 'pure and unaffected representation' did not exclude selective assimilation of the Old Master tradition of landscape painting in which Gainsborough, for whom Constable felt a particular admiration and affinity, was also steeped. The composition of both the 1802 and the 1828 Dedham landscapes was partially modelled upon *Hagar and the Angel* by Claude Lorrain, the most treasured possession of Sir George Beaumont and one of the Beaumont pictures subsequently acquired by the National Gallery in London. Sir George died in 1827 and Constable may well have decided to revive his own Claudian composition the following year as a tribute to his longstanding friend and patron.

Sir Edwin Landseer 1802–1873
Rent Day in the Wilderness

Oil on canvas, 122 × 265
Bequest of Sir Roderick
Murchison 1871
NG 586

By 1855, when he first approached Landseer with this unusual commission for a history painting, Sir Roderick Impey Murchison, President of the Royal Geographical Society and the supremely distinguished British geologist of his day, had already enlisted the assistance of two other artists in producing his own rendering of the exploits of his great-grandfather Colonel Donald Murchison. Landseer himself, then at the height of his reputation, had first visited Scotland with C.R. Leslie in 1824 when, following a momentous encounter with Sir Walter Scott, Landseer was commissioned to contribute illustrations to Cadell's edition of the Waverley novels. Landseer's impassioned enthusiasm for Scotland, which he indulged during annual shooting, hunting and sketching trips from 1825, is now popularly identified with his single most spectacular highland sporting picture, *The Monarch of the Glen*, in the collection of United Distillers.

Sir Roderick himself modelled for the figure of Colonel Murchison to whom the Jacobite Earl of Seaforth confided his Ross-shire estates after the defeat of the Old Pretender's army at Sheriffmuir in 1715 had obliged the Earl to seek refuge in Paris. The colonel in the guise of his great-grandson, is shown collecting rents from the Mackenzie tenants for his exiled master in defiance of the law while other tenants observe through telescopes the movements of a hostile party of redcoats beyond the loch. Landseer's commission was eventually delivered to his sorely tried patron in time for the Royal Academy exhibition of 1868.

Benjamin West 1738–1820 · *Alexander III of Scotland Rescued from the Fury of a Stag, by the Intrepidity of Colin Fitzgerald ('The Death of the Stag')* 1786

In 1786 West's *Alexander III* became one of the first monumental history paintings on Scottish subjects to appear on the walls of the Royal Academy in London. In 1772 the expatriate Pennsylvanian had been appointed historical painter to the king by George III who had recently commissioned a replica of his *Death of General Wolfe*, the sensation of the Academy's exhibition in the previous year. Ultimate recognition of West's vital contribution to the development of epic narrative painting in his adoptive Britain was delayed until 1792 when he succeeded Reynolds as the Academy's second president.

In 1783 Francis Humberston Mackenzie, subsequently created Lord Seaforth and Baron Mackenzie of Kintail, succeeded to the family estates and thereby to the chieftainship of the Clan Mackenzie. In his commission to West, the king's painter, in 1784 for an enormous and conspicuously expensive painted mythology, topical self-glorification was legitimised vicariously through the celebration of the heroism of Mackenzie's ancestor Colin Fitzgerald in protecting the institution of the Scottish monarchy. The reputed founder of the Clan Mackenzie, a thirteenth-century Irish exile, had sought refuge at the court of Alexander III of Scotland whose life was saved during a hunting expedition through the timely intervention of Fitzgerald. The grateful monarch having granted Fitzgerald the lands of Kintail, the Mackenzie armorial bearings incorporate a stag bleeding from the forehead in allusion to this legendary episode.

Oil on canvas, 366 × 521 Purchased with the aid of the National Heritage Memorial Fund, the National Art Collections Fund (William Lang Bequest), Ross & Cromarty District Council and Denis F. Ward 1987
NG 2448

Frederic Edwin Church 1826–1900 · *Niagara Falls, from the American Side* 1867

Oil on canvas,
257.5 × 227.3
Presented by John S.
Kennedy 1887
NG 799

Between 1848 and 1867 Church painted at least twenty views of the magnificent waterfall which is situated on the border dividing the United States and Canada and is one of the defining landmarks of north America. Based on a drawing made by Church during a visit to Niagara in July 1856 and on a sepia photograph touched with oil paint, the Gallery's picture was commissioned by the New York dealer Michael Knoedler in 1866 and may originally have been destined for inclusion in the prestigious Paris Exposition Universelle of 1867. Church had been selected to represent the United States at this critical juncture for the promotion in Europe of America's newly reaffirmed national unity following the end of the Civil War.

Church's spectacular landscapes of the Americas, Europe and the Near East enjoyed enormous popularity in the mid- to late-nineteenth century. The Gallery's picture, which made its debut in London at McLean's Gallery in the Haymarket in 1868, is the only major example of Church's work in a European public collection. At a New York sale in 1887 it was purchased for the presentation to the Scottish nation by John S. Kennedy, a Lanarkshire-born emigrant entrepreneur who had amassed a substantial fortune in iron and coal.

John Singer Sargent 1856–1925 · *Lady Agnew of Lochnaw (1865–1932)*

In 1884 the appearance of Sargent's provocative portrait of *Madame X* or *Madame Pierre Gautreau* (Metropolitan Museum, New York) caused a scandal at the Paris Salon. Having abandoned Paris for London, where he took up permanent residence, Sargent competed for fashionable patronage against the deterrent of this sudden involuntary notoriety until the early 1890s.

In 1892 the barrister Andrew Noel Agnew, who had recently inherited the baronetcy and estates of Lochnaw in Galloway, commissioned Sargent – who had recently moved from Paris – to paint his young wife Gertrude Vernon, herself the daughter of a barrister. Following the exhibition of this beguiling and highly accomplished portrait at the Royal Academy in 1898, Sargent was styled 'the Van Dyck of our times' by Auguste Rodin. From the turn of the century the American exile was lionised as painter-in-ordinary to Edwardian high society, endowed with a portrait practice comparable in status to that of Reynolds and a cult following at the Royal Academy which Sickert termed 'Sargentolatry'.

The idolisation of the artist and the adulation of his portrait launched his sitter as a society beauty who later established her own private salon in London. Ironically, the cumulative costs of sustaining celebrity with style obliged Lady Agnew to sell her own portrait to the National Gallery of Scotland in 1925.

Oil on canvas, 127 × 101
Purchased with the aid of
the Cowan Smith Bequest
Fund 1925
NG 1656

Index